the simple guide to IGUANAS

Tom Mazorlig

T.F.H. Publications, Inc.

T.F.H. Publications, Inc.
One TFH Plaza
Third and Union Avenues
Neptune City, NJ 07753

This book has been published with the intent to provide accurate and authoritative information in regard to the subject matter within. While every precaution has been taken in preparation of this book, the publisher and author assume no responsibility for errors or omissions. Neither is any liability assumed for damages resulting from the use of the information herein.

Library of Congress Cataloging-in-Publication Data
Mazorlig, Tom.
The simple guide to iguanas / Tom Mazorlig.
p. cm.
ISBN 0-7938-2118-5 (alk. paper)
1. Iguanas as pets. I. Title.
SF459.I38M29 2004
639.3'95--dc22
2003021201

www.tfh.com

Contents

Selecting Your Iguana

Give Your Iguana Some Exercise

Part One
Getting Into Iguanas

"Oh, thanks mom! I always wanted a puppy"

Introduction

Do You Really Want a Green Iguana?

I am well aware that the majority of the people who will buy and read this book already have iguanas. Hopefully, they purchased this book and their iguana at the same time and will use it to execute the proper care of their new friend.

Knowing that, I am going to take a couple of pages and talk to those of you who do not have an iguana yet. Perhaps you are thinking of getting a green iguana (also called common iguana, giant green iguana, or just plain ig or iggie) and want to find out about them before buying. Maybe a housemate wants one, and you want to know what's involved. Maybe you are just curious about them.

Green iguanas make fantastic pets as long as they are cared for properly.

Before You Buy

The following is a quick list of things you need before you bring your iguana home:

1. An appropriately sized cage

2. Proper lighting, heating, and furnishings for the cage

3. The right food

4. Agreement of the other people in your household that it's okay to have an iguana in the house

5. One or more good books on iguana care (like the one you are reading now)

6. Patience and perseverance (if you hope to have an iguana that's a nice pet)

Small aquariums are only suitable as temporary living quarters for green iguanas.

It is definitely best for you and the green iguana in question if you buy this book long before you buy the iguana. By reading this book before you have the iguana, you can make an informed choice as to whether or not an iguana is a good pet for you.

It is okay if you decide *not* to get a green iguana. They require a lot of care, and not everyone is able or willing to provide that care. In fact, few people have the love and dedication that's needed to turn a spazzy little iguana into a docile, affectionate pet (yes, iguanas can be affectionate, in their own reptilian way). You actually should feel good about this decision. After all, you've saved yourself a lot of time, money, and frustration and saved an ig from being kept by a person who is not whole-heartedly devoted to caring for him.

Most of the people who buy iguanas are not prepared to offer them all of the care and attention they need, and inevitably it is the iguana that suffers for it. In the US, up to one million iguanas arrive from farms in Latin America each year. If more than ten percent of those iguanas lived to see their first birthday, I would be surprised. This deplorable situation occurs mainly because the people buying iguanas as pets are not educated in how to care for them. Partly this is the fault of pet stores, who for years have told their customers that iguanas are easy to keep and don't get very big. However, it is also the fault of the pet keepers who did not take the time to educate themselves about iguanas.

No matter who is to blame, concerned animal lovers must do what we can to stop the carnage. I've spent many years in the pet and publishing trades trying to educate people about how to properly take care of their iguanas and other reptiles. This book is partly the result of my desire to do what little I can to stop the needless deaths of countless iguanas.

In keeping with that goal, we'll now face some hard–and sometimes unpleasant–facts about keeping iguanas. This does not mean I think that iguanas are not good pets. They are wonderful pets *when kept by dedicated, educated keepers*. I present the rougher side of life with iguanas now, so that you can figure out what you are getting into before you get into it.

Size

A full-grown iguana can be longer than a man is tall. An adult iguana requires a large cage, one that is at least 9 feet long, 5 feet wide, and 6 feet tall.

Although the change from a cute, little hatchling into an impressive, gigantic adult doesn't happen overnight, the transformation takes less time than you might imagine. A properly cared-for iguana will reach 3 feet in length by the end of his second year of life. You can expect him to be about 5 feet long at the end of the third or fourth year. This means the keeper must be ready to house a large lizard right from the beginning.

Don't think that by keeping your ig in a small cage or by feeding him less he'll stay small. That doesn't work for a person, and it won't work for an iguana. Such treatment is cruel.

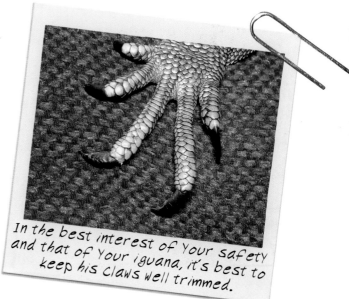

In the best interest of your safety and that of your iguana, it's best to keep his claws well trimmed.

Tooth and Claw

Iguanas come well-armed. They have strong, sharp claws and sharp teeth mounted on powerful jaws. Their tail can serve as a powerful whip. An angry or frightened iguana can be a dangerous animal.

When I say they can be dangerous, don't panic. Remember that dogs, horses, cars, power tools, and kitchen appliances will injure and kill far more people every year than iguanas ever will. I tell you about their defenses to give you some respect for an adult iguana. You should know about their capabilities before you buy one.

Environment

Iguanas come from the tropical parts of the world, and they are mostly found in rainforests and similar habitats. They spend lots of time soaking in sunlight.

This means the keeper has to provide them with a tropical environment within their enclosure. You will need heat lamps and other equipment to provide your iguana with the proper environmental conditions.

You also need to provide them with natural sunlight or a good substitute. They need certain types of ultraviolet light to stay healthy and behave normally. Bulbs that produce the correct lighting can be expensive.

Because of all the heating and lighting you must provide your iguana, expect your heating and electric bills to go up significantly.

Green iguanas are primarily vegetarians but do occasionally enjoy feedings of meat products.

Vegetarians

Iguanas are vegetarians, but this does not mean that you just feed them lettuce and fruit cocktail. You have to provide a complex, varied, and balanced diet to your green friend. This involves learning a lot about iguana nutrition, but it also involves learning about plants and their nutritional value. Every day, you'll need to give your iguana a salad composed of healthy greens and other vegetables. This requires the time to purchase (or grow) the ingredients and to wash, chop, and assemble the meal. Although fresh vegetables are not terribly expensive, the costs do add up. Iguanas eat a lot.

Taming

Iguanas are not born tame. They require a lot of handling, attention, and socializing if they are to become friendly pets. This is definitely a case in which the more you put in, the more you get back. If you spend a lot of time with your iguana and treat him with love and respect, you will have an iguana that is tame and friendly. If you only handle your iguana occasionally and keep him in the cage all of the time, you will have an iguana that views people with suspicion and fear. These are the iguanas that you hear about that bite, hiss, and whip their owners.

Lifespan

Most iguanas live less than a year. These are the ones that are getting inadequate care. A well cared-for iguana will live for at least 10 years, and lifespans of over 15 years are becoming more frequent as our knowledge of their needs has increased and the products marketed for reptiles have improved. Once you have an iguana, you have him for at least a decade, possibly close to two.

Be Realistic

I hope the previous topics caused you to start honestly thinking about your desire and ability to give a green iguana the proper care. As you read the rest of this book and learn the details, be realistic about whether or not an iguana fits into your lifestyle. Be realistic about your ability and commitment to providing proper care to an iguana for the entire span of his life.

Meet Petey and Kermit

I currently live with two iguanas, Petey and Kermit. I'll be using them as examples throughout this book, as they are the two iguanas I've lived with the longest.

Kermit is a female iguana, who is at the time of this writing approaching 13 years old. I bought her from a pet store when she was younger than six months old. I thought she was a male and she looked a bit like Kermit the Frog, hence her now gender-inappropriate name.

She has slowed down a bit from her youth and no longer can climb very well, so she is now housed by herself in a low cage. She has a nice temperament and does not bite, but she is not the most social of iguanas. This is probably because I got her in college when there seemed to always be something to do besides spend quality time with my iguana. I would do it differently now, of course.

Petey is a male iguana who is approximately ten years old. I got him when I moved into a house that a friend of mine was moving out of. My friend's wife threatened that if I did not take Petey, she was going to let him go. So, I kept him. I think I am his third owner, but it's possible I'm his fourth.

Given his background of being passed around and owned by people who didn't actually like him, Petey is not well socialized. I can now handle him a bit and enter the cage without fear of being whipped, but it took time to get to that point. When I first got him and he lived in a loft above the living room, he would flee from any approaching human. If cornered, he would fight like a dragon.

Petey's saving grace when I first took over his care was that he adored Kermit. He followed her around everywhere. He looked like a smitten teenager. It was very cute. The two of them got along for many years and even mated three seasons in a row (none of the eggs hatched, however). The last time they mated, Petey really tore up Kermit's neck, and she did not seem to want to mate that time. In the interest of her health, I reluctantly decided to separate them. She is healed now, but she bears some nasty scars.

It's been about two years since they were separated, and I think Petey still misses her. Now that she's getting on in years, I know that I'll miss her, too someday.

Salmonella

Most potential iguana owners probably have heard of salmonella (more properly called salmonellosis). Perhaps some of you have even read the news reports of whole families becoming very ill–sometimes even dying–of this illness and that the family pet iguana was the carrier of the illness. You might even have heard a neighbor, grandmother, or friend utter something like "You're getting an iguana?! They carry salmonella and it'll kill you!" Of course, this is an exaggeration of reality.

The truth of the matter is that iguanas, other reptiles, dogs, cats, birds, and other animals may indeed carry salmonella. It is also true that any of these animals can spread the illness to their keepers if the keeper handles them without some precautions. It is good to keep in mind that you are much more likely to get salmonella from eating chicken, other fowl, and eggs than you are likely to get it from your iguana or turtle.

So, what exactly is salmonella? Salmonella is a digestive illness caused by ingesting bacteria in the genera *Salmonella*. It is characterized by severe abdominal pain, fever, vomiting, and diarrhea. In very severe cases, hospitalization is required. The very young and very old are particularly vulnerable, as are people who have suppressed immune systems.

Salmonella bacteria are present in the digestive system of iguanas and many other animals. To them, salmonella are beneficial bacteria that help them digest their food. It does no good to try to eliminate the bacteria from your iguana, because it would be extremely difficult to do so and, if you were successful, your iguana's health would suffer as it would probably develop difficulty digesting food. Instead of focusing your attention on eliminating salmonella from your iguana, focus on eliminating or reducing the chance you will contract the illness.

To do this, you must first understand where the salmonella is located: in the waste material. Because the bacteria live in the digestive system, some come out at every defecation. Therefore, to avoid the bacteria, avoid the iguana's wastes. Also, avoid letting your iguana have contact with it as well. If the iguana crawls through its feces, it will surely be carrying salmonella on its skin and nails. Keeping the cage immaculate goes a long way toward preventing a salmonella infection.

The remaining tips for avoiding salmonella are mostly commonsense hygiene. Whenever you handle your iguana, wash your hands immediately afterward. Do this before you rub your eyes, bite your nails, eat, drink, or smoke. Do not eat, drink, smoke, or put your fingers in your mouth or eyes when you are cleaning the cage. Neither the iguana nor its cage furnishings should be placed on kitchen counters, dining room tables, or other food surfaces. If you use a bathtub or sink to clean the furnishings or soak the iguana, you can prevent the transmission of bacteria by soaking the tub or sink in a 10 or 20 percent bleach solution. The bleach should be allowed to soak

Always be sure to wash your hands after handling your iguana.

the surface for at least 15 minutes before rinsing. The same treatment can be given to any food surface with which the iguana accidentally comes into contact.

Given all these precautions, is it safe to have an iguana in the house with a small child? Yes, provided the care of the iguana is in the hands of those old and responsible enough to perform the cleaning, feeding, handling, and general hygiene. Very young children (meaning those approximately younger than 12, but this will vary with the child's maturity level) must be closely supervised at all times when they are interacting with the iguana. It is probably best that children younger than five or so not be allowed to handle the iguana at all.

If you suspect you have developed salmonella, don't panic. Most cases are not severe and do not require hospitalization. Remember to stay hydrated and get plenty of rest. If symptoms do not improve in 24 hours or become markedly worse, seek medical care. If at any time there is blood in the vomit or diarrhea, go to the emergency room. If a child or senior member of the household exhibits the symptoms of salmonella, it is better to seek medical care sooner rather than later.

This passage is not meant to frighten you away from keeping an iguana. It is meant to give you a realistic idea of one of the major hazards of keeping iguanas and how to avoid it. After all, forewarned is forearmed.

Meet the Green Iguana

A Look at Iguana Anatomy, Biology, and Natural History

There are a number of ways to begin our journey into iguanadom, but I will start by talking about what an iguana is and how it relates to other animals and other reptiles in particular. Then, we'll look at how the iguana lives in the wild and how his body functions. When you finish this chapter, you'll know a bit about how iguanas live in the wild and be ready to think about such an animal as a pet sharing your home.

Classification

All the known life on earth has been (or is being) classified by scientists. These classifications show

The Green Iguana, _Iguana iguana_, is Native to Tropical South America.

the relationships of one organism to another, or at least they show what we currently believe those relationships to be. The organisms are arranged in a sort of inverted pyramid. At the bottom is the species, the smallest grouping. This is the level we are speaking about when we talk about green iguanas, house cats, or human beings. As you move up the levels of the pyramid, the groupings get larger. At the top is the kingdom. These are the largest groupings of organisms. Examples of some of the different kingdoms are plants, animals, fungi, and protists (including protozoans).

Natural history of the Green Iguana

How do the green iguanas fit into this grouping? Their classification looks like this:

Kingdom: Animalia (multicellular organisms that do not produce their own food and do not have cellulose cell walls)

Phylum: Chordata (animals that have a spinal chord)

Class: Reptilia (chordate animals that lay eggs on land, have lungs, do not produce their own body heat, and share other similarities)

Order: Squamata (scaled reptiles; the snakes and lizards)

Suborder: Lacertilia (scaled reptiles that usually have eyelids and ear openings and have many skeletal similarities; the lizards)

Family: Iguanidae (the iguanas, egg-laying lizards having a particular tooth structure and other internal shared features)

Genus: *Iguana* (the green iguanas, members of the family Iguanidae that have a dewlap, a serrated crest, and other shared features)

Species: *Iguana iguana* (the common green iguana, the member of the genus having a large scale beneath the eardrum and ranging over much of Central and South America)

What does this mean for the iguana keeper? Several things. That iguanas are reptiles means that the owner must provide the iguana's heat. That they are lizards means cleaning up patches of shed skin and occasionally trimming the claws. That they are members of the genus *Iguana* means feeding them a varied, vegetarian diet and providing them with a source of ultraviolet light.

Part 1

From the classification scheme above, you could conclude that there are other types of iguanas besides the green iguana. You would be right—there is one other member of the genus. This is the Antillean iguana, scientifically known as *Iguana delicatissima*, a similar lizard found on a few islands in the lower Caribbean. It is distinguished from the green iguana by the lack of a large scale just beneath the tympanum (eardrum).

There are also several other members of the iguana family that we will just touch on here. They include the chuckwallas (genus *Sauromalus*), the desert iguana (*Dipsosaurus*), the rock iguanas (*Cyclura*), the spiny-tailed iguanas (*Ctenosaura*), Galapagos land iguanas (*Conolophus*), Galapagos marine iguanas (*Amblyrhynchus*), and the Pacific Island iguanas (*Brachylophus*). Some of these (desert iguanas, spiny-tails, some of the rock iguanas, and chuckwallas) are available in the pet trade; the rest (including many of the rock iguanas) are protected and unavailable.

The Fiji banded iguana, *Brachylophus fasciatus*, is a rare species that is endemic to the Fijian Islands.

Iguana Biology

Let's start with the basics.

Iguanas are lizards. Iguanas and all other lizards are reptiles. This means they share some common traits regarding their biology. Green iguanas also have some biological traits that are unique only to them.

To Start With…

Iguanas are diurnal lizards, meaning that they are active in the day rather than at night. They bask in the sunlight for long periods of time, warming up and absorbing ultraviolet light that they use to make vitamin D.

They are around 10 inches long from nose to tail tip when they hatch, and an adult male might be over 6 feet long. Females can reach a length between 5 and $5^{1}/_{2}$ feet. The slender tail can comprise up to two-thirds of the total length. An adult iguana may weigh over 13 pounds.

Where Do They Come From?

The green iguana is a lizard of the tropical and subtropical Americas, naturally occuring from central Mexico through most of Central America and into South America to northern Bolivia and Paraguay. The natural range also includes many near-shore islands and a few of the Caribbean islands. Through the pet trade and other human movements of the species, iguanas have spread to many areas where they did not originally occur. They now can be found on many Caribbean islands and seem to be out-competing the native Antillean iguana. Green iguanas are found in southern Florida and have probably become firmly established in breeding populations there. They are definitely established on Hawaii, and they may be causing damage to native plants and animals on those islands. This is one reason to never release your iguana into the wild: you may cause damage to the local environment.

Within this huge range, iguanas can be found in a number of habitats. They favor forests, especially those bordering rivers, streams, lakes, and other bodies of water. They can also be found in savanna, swamp, and seashore habitats, living in whatever trees are found in those areas. They adapt fairly well to the presence of man (unless over-hunted) and can be found in some surprisingly urban areas. Some parks in large cities contain decent populations of iguanas.

Tree-Dwellers

Iguanas spend much of their time high up in tree branches. The term to describe animals that live in trees is *arboreal*, and that is exactly what iguanas are. They do much of their feeding, mating, and living up in the tops of trees. They do come down to the ground occasionally, mostly to move between trees and to lay eggs. Many iguanas living near humans have learned that paved roads get very hot and make good places to bask, so they will come down to bask on the asphalt. (I nearly ran over several basking iguanas when I was in Panama. Fortunately, I never hit an iguana or any other animals.)

Iguanas tend to favor living in trees near a body of water. They like to perch on limbs that are directly

Because they are arboreal, green iguanas love to sit on tree limbs.

above the water. This is not just because iguanas like the view; the water actually is one way of avoiding danger. An iguana that feels threatened is likely to just jump off the branch and plunge into the water. Once in the water, they may swim to another area of the shore and climb a different tree, or they may just sink to the bottom. They can stay submerged for quite some time, and usually the danger will have passed by the time the iguana surfaces. Incidentally, iguanas are excellent swimmers.

When you look at an iguana, you may not think it looks like an animal that spends a lot of time climbing and living in trees. It does not have very flexible feet or opposable digits. Its tail is not prehensile. An iguana does not resemble a leaf or twig or limb. It looks mostly like any ground-dwelling lizard might.

Scientists believe the reason for this is that iguanas only recently (in a relative way, meaning several million years) developed from a terrestrial (ground-dwelling) ancestor. Almost all the other members of the family are terrestrial, and the iguana has not had time to become strongly adapted for life in the trees.

It does have one adaptation for tree-living: its claws. An iguana's claws are strong and sharp. They use them to anchor into the bark of trees. Iguanas climb very well and very fast. Their legs are powerful as well, giving them the strength to climb easily.

Despite not having many adaptations to an arboreal lifestyle, iguanas are successful animals. They occur over a wide geographical range and usually in substantial numbers. Perhaps it is because they are still generalized enough in form that they can be so successful.

However, things are not always rosy in the treetops. In their natural habitat, lots of other animals will eat iguanas if they have the chance. The juveniles have a greater number of potential predators than the adults, so iguanas grow as rapidly as they can. Some of the animals that will eat juvenile iguanas include various

The green basilisk, Basiliscus plumifrons, looks similar to green iguanas but are primarily carnivorous.

birds, snakes, larger lizards (basilisks, tegus, and others), raccoons, coatis, ocelots, margays, and monkeys.

The adults, due to their large size, have fewer predators, but they are not beyond danger. Some of the animals that prey on adult iguanas include crocodiles, boas, anacondas, jaguars, large birds of prey, and humans. Many creatures will dig up iguana nests and eat the eggs, including raccoons, coatis, humans, ants, and other lizards (primarily tegus).

Iguanas usually try to flee from danger. They will drop off their branches into water, run rapidly along the branches, or climb higher into the tree as the situation demands. If all else fails, they use their tail as a whip and have a powerful and painful bite.

Not So Cold-Blooded

Lizards, like all other reptiles and unlike mammals and birds, do not make the heat their bodies need through metabolism. They get their heat from the environment, primarily from the sun, but possibly from warmed rocks and limbs (which still means the warmth comes from the sun indirectly).

Green iguanas get their heat from their environment.

The fact that reptiles do not make their own body heat has led to the common idea that they are cold-blooded. This is not exactly true, especially when discussing desert-dwelling and tropical-dwelling lizards, like our friend the green iguana. In fact, there are some desert lizards that maintain body temperatures that average higher than a human's.

There is a commonplace idea that, for some reason, being warm-blooded is superior to being cold-blooded. Neither is really superior to the other. They are just different ways life operates. If warm-bloodedness were truly superior, you would expect there to be fewer species of cold-blooded animals and that cold-blooded animals would be being driven extinct by warm-blooded animals. That does not appear to be the case. After all, fish are cold-blooded, and there are more species of fish than there are species of birds or mammals. Some of the smallest animals (tiny fish and lizards) and some really large ones (the crocodiles) are cold-blooded. Remember that being cold-blooded is actually pretty efficient. Instead of wasting energy heating your body, you can use that energy to grow, produce young, or produce fat for lean times. The fact that reptiles are cold-blooded allows them to survive on far less food than can mammals of the same size.

Each reptile has an optimal temperature range. At this temperature, all of its body functions proceed most smoothly and efficiently. Through special behaviors and physiological adaptations, a reptile will keep its body temperature in that range as much as it can. A green iguana likes to keep its body temperature in the mid to upper 80s.

How does an iguana do this? Mostly, it uses behavior, doing certain things to raise and lower its temperature as it needs to. This is called *behavioral thermoregulation*: regulating temperature through behavior. Almost all reptiles do this, but we're just going to talk about the green iguana.

Green iguanas will move in and out of sunlight in order to regulate their body temperature.

In the morning, when an iguana is likely to be at its coldest from the nighttime drop in temperature, the first thing an iguana does is warm up. He seeks out a limb that is bathed in sunlight. The iguana will position himself in the sunlight so that the maximum amount of skin surface is exposed to the sun. He'll also darken his skin, because dark colors absorb heat more readily than light colors. As the sun moves, if the iguana is still not as warm as he'd like to be, he'll move and angle his body to continue to absorb lots of the heat of the sun.

After a while in the sun–usually an hour or so, but it depends on the air temperature and how cold the iguana got the night before–the iguana will start to get too hot. Now, he'll start using behaviors to cool himself down. He'll lighten in color, reduce the amount of his body that is exposed to the sun, and eventually he'll move out of the sun altogether.

Once the iguana is warmed up enough to be at peak speed and condition, he'll move on to his full day of foraging, running from danger, scaring off rivals, and possibly looking for mates. When he cools down too much, he'll return to the sun to warm himself back to his optimal temperature range.

Behavioral thermoregulation is important for the iguana keeper to understand. When you design your ig's cage, you must include within it opportunities for him to regulate his own temperature. Keeping him warm is not enough; he needs to have a range of temperatures to enable him to pick how warm he wants to be at that particular moment. You'll find out how to do this in the housing section.

Reptilian Cows

Iguanas are unusual for lizards in that they do not eat insects or other animals; they eat plants. There are some other lizards that, like the green iguana, are totally herbivorous, notably other members of the family Iguanidae: desert iguanas, chuckwallas, Pacific Island iguanas, marine iguanas, and Galapagos land iguanas. Some other unrelated herbivorous lizards include the spiny-tailed agamas (genus *Uromastyx*) from Africa and the Middle East and the monkey-tailed skink (*Corucia zebrata*) from the Solomon Islands.

Green iguanas will often eat broad-leafed grasses if given the chance.

In the wild, iguanas eat a variety of plants (mostly trees, shrubs, and vines) that are abundant in their area. They tend to eat the leaves of plants rather than any other parts, but some fruits and flowers are consumed. Flowers seem to be consumed mainly by juveniles, and adults eat more fruit than young. At all stages of life, however, leaves are the primary foodstuff. Very rarely, iguanas may eat animal matter in the wild (usually eggs or road-kill), but essentially they are strict herbivores.

Because iguanas eat mostly leaves, they have been called reptilian cows. This is a useful comparison, but it only goes so far. Yes, both animals eat leaves primarily, but that is about as far as the similarities go. Iguanas, unlike cows, digest the cellulose in their diet in their hindgut. Cows actually digest the cellulose of grasses in their stomachs, the foregut. There is more about iguana digestion below in the section on the digestive system and in the chapter on diet and nutrition.

Like other aspects of an iguana's body, their digestion is partially controlled by their temperature. They digest their food most efficiently at their optimal body temperature of around 85° to 87°F. At lower temperatures digestion is less efficient, and food takes longer to process and move through the body. If the temperature is very low, the food may rot in the gut before the iguana can digest it. This causes serious and often fatal illness to the iguana. If the temperature is too high, the food may pass through the digestive tract too quickly without having been fully digested. Obviously, neither situation is good for the iguana. In light of this, it makes perfect sense that iguanas tend to eat best when they are nice and warm and show little appetite when they are too cold.

The Iguana Body
Part I: The Exterior

This section is a more detailed look at the parts of an iguana and what each one does. We'll also talk about the importance of some of them in an iguana's life. Let's start at the front and work our way back.

The Nose (Snout)

Almost at the very end of an iguana's head are the nostrils. Like other animals, iguanas use their nose for breathing and for smelling. Iguanas seem to have a decent sense of smell. Like snakes, they use their tongue to gather scent molecules as well as their nose.

Small iguanas will oftentimes rub their noses on the cage.

An iguana's nostrils also contain small glands, one in each nostril. These glands act as filters of the blood, much like the kidneys. The reptilian kidney is rather poor at filtering out excess minerals from the bloodstream, yet, being herbivorous, iguanas ingest high quantities of sodium, potassium, and other minerals in their diet. The nasal gland filters out these minerals. This is why iguanas sometimes seem to snort or sneeze: they are blowing the mineral-heavy

Anatomical Words

Here are some words that will help you navigate around an iguana's body (and your own!):

Anterior: toward the head

Caudal: of or near the tail

Dorsal: of or near the back, of or near the spinal column

Lateral: the sides, away from the midline of the body

Nuchal: of or near the neck

Posterior: toward the tail

Rostral: of or near the nose (snout)

Ventral: the belly side of the body.

secretions of these glands out of their nose. This is also why iguana enclosures may have salty crusts near the iguana's favored resting spots. Cleaning salt deposits produced by these glands is just another fact of life for iguana keepers.

The Mouth

People unfamiliar with iguanas often ask if they have teeth. When I hear this question, I point to the scar on my index finger, the result of a bite by a large, unhappy male iguana. Yes, iguanas have teeth, and the teeth are adapted to easily cut through leaves (and are not bad at cutting through human skin). Iguanas lose and replace their teeth throughout their lives.

Although they have teeth, iguanas do not chew their food much. They tend to rip off a chunk of food that will fit in their mouth and swallow it. All of their teeth are more or less similar in shape, designed just to shear off pieces of leaves.

An iguana's tongue is pink, slightly forked, and highly mobile. It helps push food back into the throat. The tongue does have taste buds, but it appears that the sense of taste is not well developed in iguanas. However, the tongue helps the iguana perceive scents. Like a snake, an iguana will flick its tongue out into the air and onto surfaces. The tongue picks up scent molecules and transports them to the roof of the mouth.

In the roof of the mouth is a specialized organ, Jacobson's organ. This is a tissue-lined indentation in the palate that has special receptors, similar to the scent receptors in the nose. From these receptors, nerve cells transport scent information to the brain. The Jacobson's organ seems to be more sensitive than the nose in detecting scent.

The Eyes

Like humans, iguanas are visual creatures, and vision is easily their most important sense. Their eyes are very sensitive, able to pick out motion and detail with great accuracy. It may come as a surprise to some that iguanas can see colors. In fact, there is some evidence that they see color even better than humans do. Actually, quite a few lizards that often feed on flowers and fruits have good color vision and even have color preferences–yellow, red–among the flowers that are eaten. The next time someone tells you that animals can't see color, tell him or her that.

An iguana's eyes are located on the upper sides of the head. This gives excellent lateral vision, some rear vision, and a little bit of binocular vision directly in front of their heads. Their excellent lateral vision is the reason that iguanas look at interesting things by turning their heads. They line up the item they want to see with one of their eyes to see it best.

Like many birds and some other lizards, iguanas have a ring of small bones, the scleral ossicles, embedded in the outer surface of the eye, forming a ring around the eye itself. These ossicles give some support to the eye and also may help protect it from run-ins with twigs while an iguana is moving quickly.

The Tympanum (Eardrum)

Slightly above and just behind the corner of the jaw on an iguana, you will notice a flattened, semi-transparent scale. This is actually not a scale but the iguana's eardrum, more properly called a tympanum. There is no separate outer-ear structure to concentrate and localize sounds, as found in mammals, but instead the tympanum is open to the outside and just slightly below the level of the scales of the side of the head. Under the tympanum is a small cavity called the middle ear, which leads to the deeply embedded inner ear cavity that contains the organs of balance, hearing, and motion-detection.

The subtympanic plate is the large scale located just below the tympanic scale.

Iguanas seem to hear fairly well but probably not as well as humans. Still, they react readily to strange and threatening noises. Because of this, you may want to avoid exposing your iguana to loud or obnoxious sounds (loud stereos and televisions) or sudden loud noises. When your iguana is sleeping, respect that and keep your entertainment volume down.

One reason green iguanas extend their dewlaps is to make them appear larger than they actually are.

The iguana inner ear has fluid-filled tubes that monitor the position of the head, thus allowing the iguana to maintain his orientation and balance. Iguanas that have inner ear infections act the same as a human with an inner ear infection: they cannot balance themselves and may become nauseous.

The Subtympanic Plate (Cheek Scale)

Just below and behind the level of the tympanum, at the corner of the lower jaw, there is an enlarged and glossy scale. This is the subtympanic plate (from *sub*- meaning *below*, the tympanum). You may also see it referred to as the subtympanic scale or subtympanic shield, or, more generally, the "cheek scale."

The function of this scale is not certain, but it is the major difference between green iguanas, which have the scale, and Antillean iguanas, which do not. It could be a false eye to confuse predators or might play a role in the social behavior and communication between iguanas. It also might have no real function. In many iguanas the subtympanic plate is broken into two to five (rarely more) smaller scales, but it always is easily distinguished. It often is raised in the center.

The Dewlap

Under an iguana's chin are folds of skin that extend into a rounded, flag-like structure when the iguana is excited, angry, or upset. This is the dewlap or gular fold. Males have much larger dewlaps than females.

At the leading edge of the dewlap is a spine of cartilage. This is an extension of the hyoid bone, which supports the dewlap and enables it to fold up or down. The rest of the hyoid is embedded in the tongue and floor of the mouth and serve mostly to give the tongue mobility.

The extended dewlap makes an iguana look bigger and more frightening, helping to scare off predators and rivals. The dominant iguana in a group will often keep his dewlap extended, while the subordinates will keep theirs relaxed, pulled back toward the throat.

The dewlap also may play a role in thermoregulation. When an iguana is cool, it can inflate its dewlap while it basks. This increases the surface area of the animal exposed to the sunlight.

The Crest
Along the spine of an iguana, you will see flattened, pointed, finger-like projections of scales forming a line from the nape to the base and sometimes end of the tail. These make up the iguana's crest. You can refer to the crest as having three different areas: the nuchal (neck) crest, the dorsal (back) crest, and the caudal (tail) crest. The crests of males are larger and more developed than the crests of females.

> ### What Kind of Therm Are You?
> There are two scientific terms for the two ways animals heat themselves. Animals that generate their own heat (birds and mammals) are called *endotherms* (*endo-* means "inside" or "within"). Animals that get their heat from the outside environment are called *ectotherms* (*ecto-* means "outside"). Those terms are good to know, as you will come across them when you do more reading on reptiles.

The projections of the crest are soft and flexible. They are not spines or spikes (although even experienced iguana-keepers will sometimes call them that), despite this common misconception. Iguanas sometimes damage these projections. They grow back, but very slowly and often do not look normal compared to other projections.

The function of the crest is unknown. The most accepted theory now is that the crest helps an iguana look larger than it actually is. Some have suggested that the crest helps break up the outline of the iguana, helping it to remain unnoticed by predators. It also may have something to do with the sexes recognizing each other, and perhaps it even has a part in thermoregulation.

Legs, Feet, and Claws
The robust legs of an iguana are splayed out to the side like those of all other living reptiles that have legs. The legs have a thick, stocky look to them, an indication that they are very strong and muscular.

Iguanas use their legs for running—and they are fast—and climbing, at which they excel, along with normal walking. They also use their legs for scratching, much as does a dog or cat. When at rest, an iguana's legs are usually folded along its side or dangled down from the branch it rests upon (although they prefer to rest on branches that are wider than their body).

There is one especially interesting feature of the hind legs. On the underside of your ig's thighs, you may notice a row of small pores. They are more visible in adult iguanas and may be invisible on a baby. These are the femoral pores. The pores on an adult male are much larger than the ones on the female. The male's pores secrete a wax-like material that is thought to be used as a territorial marker when rubbed onto a branch or trunk.

An iguana's feet are not very flexible, and they cannot use them to grasp or carry anything. There are five front digits and five rear digits, usually called toes. The toes cannot move fully independently, being partially enclosed in skin at their bases. However, each of the long toes ends in a long, curved, sharp claw. The claws are the iguana's major adaptation to a life spent high in the trees. Indeed, if you did not see the claws, you might not even realize that iguanas are arboreal. The sharpness and sturdiness of the claws enable iguanas to ascend trees (and curtains and pants legs) with incredible speed.

Although an iguana does not use its legs to lash out with the claws in defense, the claws can cause severe lacerations if the iguana flails about, such as when you are trying to restrain it during a vet exam. It is wise to keep your iguana's claws trimmed.

The Vent

This area of the body has a name for what it does: it vents out the wastes that the iguana produces. Unlike mammals but like birds and fish, reptiles have one opening that is used for feces, urine, and reproductive products (eggs). The vent more properly should be referred to as the cloaca, which refers to the sewage canals of ancient Rome that carried wastes from the homes to the sea.

The vent is on the underside of the iguana, just behind the legs, at the base of the tail. It appears as a more-or-less horizontal slit with swollen edges.

The Tail

Most of the length of an iguana is composed of its tail. This gives you some indication of how important the tail is to the life of the iguana. The tail, assuming no part of it has been lost, will be one-half to two-thirds the total length of the iguana. Though thick at the base, it soon becomes distinctly flattened from side to side (laterally compressed). As you move down the length of the tail, it tapers to a fine, whip-like end.

The base of the tail is usually green like the rest of the iguana. Along its length, it becomes more and more thickly banded with brown. Eventually, the tail is completely brown.

It may surprise you that his tail is an iguana's first line of defense against predators (not counting running away). An iguana that is seriously threatened will position his body sideways, inflate himself to look as big as possible, and draw back his tail. If the threatening creature doesn't take the hint, the iguana will lash his tail with terrific speed and power. A smack from the tail will cause great pain to most creatures. There are anecdotal reports–which I don't doubt–of dogs losing eyes to the lash of an iguana's tail. In humans (and other soft-skinned animals), an iguana's tail can caused raised and sometimes bleeding welts.

Aside from defense, an iguana's tail helps it to balance when it climbs and leaps. When an iguana takes to the water, the tail is a powerful propellant as well as a rudder.

Many lizards exhibit an adaptation called tail *autotomy*. This means the tail can easily break off from the body. This serves as an anti-predatory strategy. If a predator grabs the tail, it breaks off and the lizard escapes. In most species that have tail autotomy, the tail continues to thrash around after it separates from the body. This helps keep the predator's attention while the lizard runs for cover. The tail regrows, although species vary in how quickly it regrows, how hindered the lizard is until it regenerates, and in how normal the regrown tail appears.

In nature, it seems that lizards that lose their tails have lower survivorship than lizards that do not. Thus, although it is better to lose your tail to a predator than to lose your life, it is best not to lose your tail at all.

Iguanas are a species with tail autotomy. However, it must be noted that breaking off and regrowing the tail are not simple tasks. Regrowing the tail costs the iguana metabolic resources. The stub end must be protected from infection; it is an open wound, after all. Most iguanas do not grow back perfect tails. They are usually stunted, misshapen, and off-colored. Though juveniles tend to regrow their tails better than adults, regrowing a tail may cost a juvenile some growth. Youngsters that should be spending all their energy on growing now have to spend considerable energy growing a new tail. This may cost them some growth or compromise them in other ways. It certainly seems to stress them out.

Soaking your green iguana helps to ease the shedding of dead skin.

Now that you've read this, you probably realize you should never hold your iguana by his tail.

The Scales

Covering the iguana from nose to the tip of the tail are his scales. Iguanas are said to have heterogeneous scales. That is, the scales vary in size and structure on different parts of the body. This should come as no surprise if you've ever looked closely at an iguana before. You should be able to see several different types of scales easily.

Some of the different scales have been mentioned already. There are the spine-like projections of the crest and the subtympanic scale. You may also notice that on the neck of the iguana, especially in an adult, there are a number of hard, pointed, conical scales. These are sometimes called tuberculate scales. These scales help protect an iguana's neck from bites, both from predators and from other iguanas. The scales on the bottom of the feet and the underside of the thigh have some roughened surfaces. These may help iguanas to climb.

The scales function much the same as the outer coatings of other animals. They hold in moisture, protect the inside of the animal from the sun's radiation, protect it from injury, and protect it from disease. The scales are just specialized skin cells, formed into a hardened covering.

Shedding

Throughout an iguana's life, it will periodically shed its skin. Unlike snakes, which usually shed in one piece, iguanas shed in patches.

Younger iguanas that are growing rapidly shed more often than the adults. Iguanas that have recently gained or lost a lot of weight or had some kind of skin ailment usually will start a new shed cycle.

When your iguana is getting ready to shed, his colors will be more dull and subdued. Your ig may get a grayish or bluish tinge. Right before he sheds, you may notice tiny white spots. These are normal, not fungal infections or mites.

Shortly after the white spots appear, some patches of skin will begin to peel or flake off. If you are keeping your iguana humid enough, he will shed easily without your help. Occasionally, shed skin will stick to a spine or to the tip of the tail. If you are observing your iguana closely on a regular basis, you will spot these bits. Gently remove them as discussed in the section on grooming.

Some iguanas get moody during a shed. They may eat less (rarely, they'll eat more), get cranky, or become restless. It varies with the individual iguana.

Part II: The Interior

Now that we've discussed all of the parts of the iguana we can see, let's move on to those we can't see. These are no less important for the iguana owner to know about, as they play just as vital a role in your iguana's life and health as the external bits.

Skeletal System

The skeletal system of iguanas carries out the same functions as it does in other animals. It serves as protection, framework, a point for the muscles to act on in movement, and a reservoir of minerals for use in the body.

When an iguana is fed a poor diet or not allowed access to ultraviolet light, metabolic bone disease develops, causing weakness and malformation of the bones. See the sections on diet and lighting for more information.

The skull of an iguana is rather large and heavily calcified, with large openings for the eyes (orbits) and the nostrils. There is a pair of large openings behind the eyes on each side of the skull that allows the muscles of the jaws to attach to the skull for support and leverage; these are the temporal fossae. The teeth, which number about 30 on each side above

Small iguanas need a well-balanced diet and good care to grow into big iguanas.

Iguanas have Three Eyes?

Well, sort of. On top of the head, between the eyes, is a small, translucent scale. This scale covers what is called the parietal eye. Beneath it is a sensory nerve that detects light and dark only, not actual images. The nerve runs deep into the brain to the pineal gland.

The parietal eye is stimulated by light and seems to serve two functions. One function is to detect sudden changes in the light coming from overhead—such as when the shadow of a predatory bird passes by. The other function is to provide information on the amount of sunlight an iguana is getting. This allows the iguana to move in and out of shade as it needs to (thus preventing overheating) and detects the changing of the seasons.

Thus, the parietal scale acts both as an eye and as a type of body calendar.

and 25 on each lower jaw, are placed on the inside of each jaw (pleurodont) and have rather long shafts and triangular crowns with sharp edges used for shearing leaves. The teeth are constantly replaced from below by new teeth. The upper teeth are borne on the maxillary bone except for the first few that are placed on the fused premaxillary bones. The anterior-most teeth are more fang-like than the rest of the teeth and can produce deep wounds, while the other teeth produce cuts. The lower jaws are large, with a high process (the coronoid) that serves as a muscle insertion point posteriorly. The teeth of the lower jaw arise from the dentary bone.

As in most other vertebrates, the vertebral column of an iguana is comprised of many vertebrae, which have processes to the sides that attach to ribs, dorsal (neural) processes that bear ligaments and sheath the spinal chord, and special articulating surfaces and processes that allow the vertebrae to join with each other and flex in almost any direction to some extent. There are eight cervical (neck) vertebrae, 16 thoracolumbar (trunk) vertebrae, two sacral (anchoring to the pelvis) vertebrae, and many slender caudal (tail) vertebrae. The first two cervical vertebrae are modified as an atlas and axis that allow the head to move freely, as in mammals. The vertebrae (except for the atlas and axis) have a concave anterior surface and a convex, ball-like posterior surface, allowing very free movement. Almost every vertebra of the neck and trunk (as well as the basal tail vertebrae) can be identified and put into its proper place in the backbone by noticing the development of the various processes and articulating surfaces.

The sternum of an iguana is largely cartilaginous with some secondary bone and is relatively slender. It serves as attachment for the ribs and also for the pectoral girdles, which articulate with the front legs through the coracoids or collarbones. The pelvis is simple but contains the same paired ilium (dorsal), pubis (front), and ischium (at the back) as mammals. A large cavity, the acetabulum, provides articulation with the femur of the upper leg. As in most higher vertebrates, each front leg consists of the humerus of the upper leg and the paired radius and ulna of the lower, articulating with the phalanges (toes) over the bones of the wrist. The back leg consists of the heavy femur of the upper leg and the paired tibia and fibula of the lower leg, connecting to the phalanges of the toes through a few bones in the ankles.

Brain and Nervous System

On the surface, the brain and nervous system of green iguanas do not differ markedly from those of other vertebrates: there is a skull-enclosed brain in the head and a bone-enclosed spinal cord running down the back of the animal; other nerves radiate out from these two structures. The nerves control most functions of the body, including movement, reflex arcs, responses to various stimuli, and perception.

Iguanas have all the familiar senses: sight, hearing, smell, taste, and touch. They certainly can feel pain. They react faster when warm than when cool, which is true of many tropical reptiles.

There has not been much research done on the intelligence of green iguanas. From my own observations and what others have told me, I believe iguanas are intelligent for reptiles. They will never win a chess game, but they are more aware and interactive than most snakes, geckos, and other herps. I do not think they are as intelligent as most monitor lizards, which seem to be the brightest lizards. However, iguanas do have personalities, they seem to have a limited capacity for planning, and they do remember things. If you think your iguana smeared poop all over his cage because he was mad at you for not taking him outside today, you are probably right. There are some keepers who claim their iguanas respond to their names and some basic commands.

Digestive System

The digestive system of an iguana is adapted to a diet composed completely of plant matter. More specifically, it's adapted to a diet of leaves. This has involved the development of several specializations.

Food passes from the mouth to the esophagus, where muscular contractions push it down to the stomach. The acids and enzymes in the stomach break down the food chemically, while muscular contractions break it down mechanically. Additionally, the contractions

SVL

Most scientists and veterinarians measure lizards not from nose to tail tip, but from the nose to the vent. This is called the snout-vent length, abbreviated SVL. The reason they use the snout-vent length as the standard it that this length is not affected by the condition of the tail. For example, if an iguana has a run-in with a predator (or a rocking chair), it could lose a lot of its tail. His overall length would change, but it's SVL would remain the same. Therefore, measuring from nose to tail-tip would provide a deceptive picture of how big the animal actually is. The snout-vent length is a more accurate measurement. In this book, I'll mostly be using measurements to the end of the tail, but I wanted to make you aware of the SVL, so you could make sense of other publications on iguanas and other herps.

help mix the food and the acid-enzyme stew together, making sure all parts of the food are exposed to the stomach's chemicals.

From the stomach, the food passes to the small intestine. Here, the stomach acids are neutralized and more enzymes (some from the pancreas and liver) go to work breaking it down chemically. The small intestine absorbs water and nutrients from the food and passes them to the blood stream.

When the food leaves the small intestine, it travels to the hindgut (colon). It is here that iguanas digest the cellulose in the plants they eat (the cell walls of plant cells are composed primarily of cellulose). Humans have a very limited ability to digest cellulose, and most of the cellulose humans eat passes through the digestive tract, performing a valuable cleaning function as dietary fiber but not actually being digested. In iguanas, the cellulose is actually digested and rendered into important nutrients.

In the hindgut, an iguana plays host to a great number of species of bacteria and protozoans (and possibly also some fungi and nematodes). These microbes do not harm the iguana; actually, they are highly beneficial. It is these organisms that actually digest the cellulose, transforming it into usable nutrients for the iguana. These nutrients include proteins, several vitamins, and fatty acids that are absorbed by the specialized hindgut.

Once the food passes from the hindgut, most of what is left is waste. It journeys to the rectum, where some water will be absorbed. From the rectum, the feces exit the body from the vent.

Endocrine System

The endocrine system regulates in some way almost all activities of the body through the use of chemical messengers, the hormones. Iguanas have nearly the same endocrine glands as humans, and they produce similar hormones. Of course, there are differences in the iguana versions and the human versions of these hormones, but they perform the same functions. Both human and iguana insulins stimulate the body's cells to absorb sugars, for example. Because of the great number of endocrine glands and the diverse roles they play in normal body function, only a few will be touched on here.

The pituitary gland is called the master gland. Its major function is to regulate the other endocrine organs and make sure they are doing their jobs. It is particularly important in the regulation of growth, reproduction, and the absorption of water by the kidneys. It is a small organ that sits above the palate and just beneath the brain.

The pineal gland is a poorly understood gland, even in humans. It rests deep in the brain and seems to be involved in regulating cycles of sleeping and waking.

Sitting in the throat, approximately at the level of the larynx, the thyroid gland is responsible for the regulation of metabolism. As in humans, the hormones the thyroid gland produces require iodine in their manufacture. If you feed your iguana properly, he will receive all the iodine he needs. Some plants (cabbage, broccoli, and their relatives) can interfere with thyroid function. See the chapter on nutrition for more information.

The parathyroids are tiny glands embedded within the thyroid glands. They have a function distinct from that of the thyroid, the regulation of the levels of calcium and phosphorus in the bloodstream. This has important implications for an iguana's growth and health. If the hormones involved are not in proper balance, skeletal weakness and malformation can result. Exposure to natural sunlight and a proper diet will ensure that the function of these two hormones is normal.

When an iguana needs to respond to stress, its adrenal glands go to work. They produce adrenaline and other hormones that ready the body for flight or fight. They cause the muscles to react faster and more strongly, the heart and lungs to pump faster, and other changes necessary for a rapid response in a life-threatening situation. They also inhibit areas of the body not needed during an emergency, including the digestive and immune systems. An iguana constantly in a stressful situation (nowhere to hide in his cage; constantly being bothered by children in the home) keeps producing adrenaline. Eventually this causes disease, as the iguana is not fighting off infection very well and has

A boy or a girl?

Telling male iguanas from female iguanas is very simple when you are looking at adults and nearly impossible when you are looking at babies. Baby iguanas do not have the secondary sexual characteristics that make the adults' sexes easily identifiable.

Adult males get larger than females and have larger jowls, dewlaps, and dorsal crests. At the base of the tail, the male iguana appears to be swollen. These are the hemipenal bulges, and this is where the male keeps his paired hemipenes when they are not in use. On the underside of the thighs, there is a row of small pores. An adult male's pores will be much larger than in a female. The pores of males usually excrete a thick, waxy material that is probably used as some form of territorial marking. Additionally, male iguanas in the breeding season often get an orange flush to their heads, forelimbs, and forequarters.

In babies and juveniles, there is no accurate way to tell the sexes apart. It may be possible to "pop" male iguanas (using pressure on the base of the tail to make the hemipenes pop out of the vent), but this requires a very skilled and gentle person and some luck. If the iguana is incorrectly popped, damage to the tail, pelvis, or hemipenes may result. You definitely want an experienced person doing this to avoid any harm to your baby.

If you are buying a baby and you are trying to buy one of a certain sex, look at the group of iguanas. The most brightly colored ones are often males. Look also at the dewlap and the crest; those with the largest dewlaps and crests have the best chance of being males. Finally, look at the base of the tail. Some baby and juvenile males have a hint of a hemipenal bulge.

There is a good chance you will pick out the opposite sex than the one you wanted. By the time you find this out, you will have had your iguana for at least a year and hopefully will love it enough so the sex will not matter. Then you can join the ranks of iguana owners who have igs with gender-inappropriate names!

an upset digestive system. The adrenal glands are located in the tissue that supports the ovaries and testes of an iguana, not near the kidneys as in many other animals.

Heart and Circulatory System

One of the differences between reptiles and mammals mentioned in biological texts is that reptiles have a three-chambered heart and mammals have a four-chambered heart. The extra chamber in the mammals ensures that the oxygen-rich blood from the lungs and oxygen-poor blood from the body do not mix. In some older texts, it is often cited as one way in which mammals are superior to reptiles. Recently, some research has shown that, through muscular contractions within the heart and the timing of bloodflow, the oxygen-rich blood and oxygen-poor blood do not mix in reptiles either, another blow to the theory of mammalian superiority.

In any case, iguanas have a heart, arteries, veins, and capillaries just like other vertebrates. The blood carries nutrients and oxygen to the tissues and takes away carbon dioxide and metabolic wastes to be eliminated. The circulatory system is one of the major parts of the immune system, as some blood cells function in the identification and destruction of disease-causing organisms. In iguanas and other reptiles, the red blood cells still possess a nucleus, which is absent in mammals.

The circulation also functions in the distribution of heat through the body of your iguana. This is important considering that the body cannot make its own heat. Often you may see your iguana seem to be basking just his head. In nature, this behavior helps prevent predation. By having only his head in the light, the iguana is less likely to be seen than if its whole body were in the patch of sun. The brain gets warm soonest, and having the brain working at optimal condition and speed is important. Because of blood circulation, the rest of the body will still get warm as well.

Reproductive System

Reptiles, including iguanas, have all of their reproductive organs on the inside of the body; there are no normally exposed external genitalia. This can make sexing young iguanas challenging, but the sexing of adults is easy because of the many secondary sexual characteristics.

The primary organ of the female reproductive system is called the ovary, just as in mammals and other animals. There are two ovaries located in the body cavity above the kidneys. The ovaries produce the various female sex hormones and the egg cells, or ova (singular: ovum). Each ovary has a tube-like oviduct leading from it. After release from the ovary, the ovum moves

Male green iguanas exhibit a slight bulge at the base of their tail.

into the oviduct. Here, it can be fertilized by the sperm. Special membranes are added, encapsulating the zygote (term for a recently fertilized ovum). The outermost membrane is calcified and hardens, becoming the eggshell. The eggs are stored in the oviduct (in an enlarged area sometimes called the uterus) until the mother iguana lays them in a nest.

In the male, the primary sexual organs are the testes or testicles (singular: testis). There are two of these, located above the kidneys just like the ovaries in the female. These organs produce male sex hormones and produce and store the sperm cells. It should be noted that iguanas have some of the largest testes relative to body size in the entire animal kingdom. It really isn't any wonder that male iguanas in the breeding season can think of nothing else besides mating!

Male iguanas do not have a typical penis or intromittent organ. Instead, they have a deeply divided, virtually paired organ at the base of the tail called the hemipenis or hemipenes. When the male becomes sexually excited, one (rarely both) of the hemipenes becomes engorged with blood and inflates out of the vent (it sort of turns inside out in the process). During mating, one of the hemipenes is inserted into the vent of the female.

Sperm released from the testes travel down into a groove on the hemipene. As they travel, secretions from other glands are added; the product of the mixture is called seminal fluid or semen. If the male is mating, the semen goes from the hemipenis into the vent of the female. From there, the sperm swim up the female's oviducts and fertilizes any ova that might be present.

Herps is the Word

Throughout this text I'll be using the term *herps* to refer to reptiles and amphibians collectively. This word comes from the word *herpetology*, which is the study of reptiles and amphibians. Some use the word *herptile,* but I feel this term stresses reptiles over amphibians, so I choose not to use it. When speaking of the hobby of keeping reptiles and amphibians, I will usually call it the *herp hobby. Herpetoculture* is the keeping and breeding of reptiles and amphibians. A *herper* is someone who participates in the herp hobby or herpetoculture.

Respiratory System

Iguanas have most of the same parts of their respiratory system as we have in ours: two lungs, bronchi, glottis, ribs, and rib muscles (called the intercostal muscles). What we have that iguanas lack is a diaphragm, the muscular disc at the bottom of the ribs that generates most of the motion for breathing. Instead of a diaphragm, iguanas and other lizards rely on the motions of the rib muscles to provide the force for breathing.

A Word on Scientific Names

You may have noticed that sometimes animals are referred to by strange, alien-sounding names. Perhaps you've seen these alien words in italics following the name of an animal you recognize (for instance, the house cat is known as *Felis domesticus*). These are scientific names and are used by scientists and other animal professionals to exactly identify the animals they are talking about. You may be thinking, "Why not just use the regular name?" The reasons for this are several. One is so scientists from all over the world—with different native languages—have one name for each animal (and plant and fungus, and so on). If you search under a scientific name on the Internet, you will get results in many languages (which may or may not be helpful), but if you search under the regular, or common, name, you may not get any non-English results. Another reason is that one animal may have several common names, varying by region or culture. For example, the ball python is commonly called the royal python in England, but it's scientific name, *Python regius*, is the same all over the world. Lastly, one common name may refer to more than one animal. If you are talking about green treefrogs, you might mean the species commonly called the green treefrog or you could be speaking about a number of other species of treefrogs that happen to be green. But if you are talking about the American green treefrog, you can call it *Hyla cinerea* and avoid any confusion.

How does each animal get a scientific name? Whenever a person discovers a new animal and formally describes in a scientific paper how this animal is different from similar ones, that scientist gives it a scientific name. Each name has two parts. The genus or generic name is the first part and always starts with a capital letter. A genus is a group of closely related species sharing several characteristics. Thus, most of the pythons are in the genus *Python* and most small cats are in *Felis*. The second part of the name is the species or specific name. Each combination of genus and species name is unique and describes only one animal (i.e., *Python regius, Felis domesticus).* The generic and specific names are always italicized (or underlined) to allow for easier recognition of the names of animals being discussed in a paper. After you use the whole name of a species once in a written discussion, you can just abbreviate the genus when you use it later (i.e., *P. regius, F. domesticus*).

Sometimes, a scientific name has a third part. This is called the subspecies or subspecific name. Subspecific names are used when two groups of organisms are different but not so different as to recognize two species. Usually this happens when two groups of one species are somewhat isolated from each other geographically and differences develop. As an example, the Jackson's chameleon has three subspecies: *Chamaeleo jacksoni jacksoni, C. j. merumontanus*, and *C. j. xantholophus*. Notice that the species name can be abbreviated like the generic name when discussing subspecies.

This pertains to iguanas because they—like all other organisms—have a scientific name: *Iguana iguana*. The closely related and similar looking Antillean iguana is known as *I. delicatissima*. There used to be a subspecies of iguana recognized as *I. i. rhinolopha*, denoting the iguanas that had a horn-like scale on the snout. It was once believed that only Central American iguanas developed this characteristic, but it was later discovered that individual iguanas from practically anywhere within the range could exhibit the faux horn, and therefore, it did not indicate a discrete subspecies. Currently no subspecies of green iguana is recognized, though some workers feel that eventually several subspecies could be recognized.

An iguana can hold its breath for quite some time. They can do this when under water or just when they feel the need. It is often a reaction to stress, and it may help them to remain still, keeping the eye of a predator from spotting them. They may even react to unwanted attention by doing this, releasing the breath in a great, big *huff.* Incidentally, iguanas can partially shut off the bloodflow to their lungs when they are diving.

Iguanas will sometimes breathe with their mouths open. Normally, this indicates your iguana is a little too warm and is trying to cool himself. However, if the breathing seems labored or is accompanied by other signs of distress, you must move quickly to figure out what the problem is and/or call an emergency vet. If your iguana seems to be coughing or sneezing (not just blowing out salt from his nasal glands), he probably has a respiratory infection and needs to see a vet immediately.

Where Do I Get an Iguana?

Once you've decided that an iguana is indeed the pet for you and that you are committed to the proper care of this large, long-lived animal, it's time to decide where to get one. Most people probably think first of going to the pet store to buy an iguana. Of course, you can get an iguana at most pet stores, but there are a few other places where you may find one. Each source of iguanas has its associated pluses and minuses that you should be aware of before deciding on one.

The Private Breeder

Unfortunately, very few private individuals breed iguanas. It requires hefty investments of time, space, and money to be successful at breeding

Green iguanas are available from a wide variety of sources.

From Farm to Pet Store

Most of the iguanas in pet stores have made a harrowing journey from farms in Central or South America. These are the details in brief.

Iguanas are rounded up at the farms and placed in sacks, usually about seven to a bag.

The bags are put into small boxes and these into larger boxes. All told, several dozen iguanas may be in the box for days.

The boxes are driven to airports and loaded onto planes bound for the United States, Europe, and other countries that import iguanas.

They arrive at the importer and are either unpacked or shipped directly to wholesalers. By this time, they have probably spent several days in their bags.

When they are unpacked at the importer or wholesaler, they are generally crammed into crowded cages. Lighting, heating, watering, and feeding are usually inadequate.

One or several iguanas are then bagged up again and shipped to a pet store.

Once at the pet store, they may or may not be overcrowded and improperly cared for, depending on whether the pet store cares about the animals it sells and whether or not anyone working there knows anything about iguanas.

Knowing this, it is no wonder why so many iguanas fail to thrive for their owners. Even if the owner gives one proper care, the iguana may be so injured, stressed, or ill that it cannot recover. Providing the appropriate housing and diet right from the start is key in establishing a freshly imported iguana, as is a visit to a herp vet within the first few weeks of purchase.

and raising iguanas, and there is little financial incentive to do so. Because iguanas are imported in such massive numbers from farms and wild habitats, the price on these lizards is so low that private breeders cannot compete.

If you are lucky enough to find someone who breeds iguanas, this is the best source for obtaining your iguana. A private breeder is obviously someone who cares greatly about iguanas, so the iguanas they are offering for sale (or adoption if you are really lucky and the person is a real iguanophile) will almost certainly be in top condition. What is more, the breeder is likely to be able to tell you about the temperaments of the individual babies, exactly what they have been eating, any relevant health issues, and a host of other information a new owner may find useful.

The iguana itself will not have been stressed by capture, shipment, time spent in inadequate conditions, poor diet, and overcrowding. It will have had little or no opportunity to pick up parasites or diseases. It is likely the iguana will have been handled by the breeder and be accustomed to people; this will be a big jump-start in your efforts to socialize your pet.

Where do your find one of these wonderful breeders? Well, it isn't easy. If you have a local herp society, there may be a member who breeds iguanas or a member may know of an iguana breeder. You can check on the various reptile and iguana Internet forums and bulletin boards. You can call local animal shelters and pet stores to see if anyone at one of these places knows of a breeder. Reptile expos might have a vendor who breeds iguanas or a vendor who knows someone who does. Clearly, if you want an iguana that was definitely captive-bred, you will have to do some serious detective work.

Reptile Expos

If you are not already a reptile aficionado, you may never have heard of a reptile expo (also called reptile shows, herp expos, or herp shows). These events, which take place in almost every state at various times of the year, are gatherings of vendors selling reptiles and related supplies. At some of these shows, local herp societies and herp adoption agencies may have booths or tables.

Some expos are for captive-bred animals only. At these shows you are unlikely to find iguanas (as we have discussed, few people breed iguanas). Most shows allow a mix of captive-bred, farm-raised, and wild-caught animals. These are the shows at which you are most likely to find iguanas.

Whence Comes My Iguana?

Iguanas are imported into the US from a number of different countries. Among the two largest exporters currently are El Salvador and Colombia. Some of the largest farms are in these countries. However, there are several other countries that export iguanas, including Honduras, Surinam, and Guyana. In the past, most of the countries that have iguanas have exported them, so there may still be some adults out there from Mexico or Nicaragua, for instance.

Central American iguanas are generally brownish or orangish as adults and very green in the hatchlings. They tend to be more slender than the iguanas of South America and are more likely to have a horn-like scale or scales on the snout.

South American iguanas are less orange and more often bluish as adults. They tend to be stockier than Central American iguanas.

Of course, because iguanas come from such a huge range, there are numerous minor and inconsistent regional differences.

There are several advantages to buying an iguana at an expo. You will usually be able to peruse the iguanas offered by several vendors in one place, so the selection will be great. Prices at expos are normally very good, so your iguana may cost you less than in a pet store. You will likely be able to buy any supplies you might need at the same time you buy your iguana, and expos are good sources of herp-specific supplies that pet stores may not carry.

There are also disadvantages of buying an iguana at an expo. The iguanas are likely to be crowded into a small cage, even on the table of caring and reputable vendors. Space on the tables is limited. The iguanas probably will lack adequate heat and light, so determining the health of an individual may be difficult. Also, the iguanas will not be in the best of moods. They will be stressed and scared by the strange surroundings and the hustle and bustle around their container. Even one that is normally tame may be a nervous wreck or aggressive demon at an expo. Even given this situation, you should attempt to handle a few before making your selection. If a vendor refuses to let you handle them, walk away and look elsewhere, as this vendor is either rude or has something to hide.

Reptile expos are listed in the herp magazines and at various online bulletin boards. If one is coming particularly close to your area, the local paper may also list it in a local events section.

Pet Stores

The vast majority of iguana owners obtain their iguanas at a pet store. Most pet stores sell iguanas, so locating one near you should not be too difficult.

The iguanas at pet stores are usually farm-raised babies from tropical South America–Colombia and El Salvador, most frequently. They have traveled very far under adverse conditions, so their health may be an issue. A conscientious pet store will sell only healthy ones and give all of the iguanas they have proper care.

If you are buying your iguana from a pet store, I advise you to shop around. Check out several pet stores and make note of several things: Do they sell a variety of reptiles (good) or just iguanas and one or two species (not as good)? Are the iguanas in clean, roomy cages with correct heating and lighting? Are there dead iguanas in the cage? (If you see iguanas that did not die recently, this is a very bad sign.) Do the other animals look healthy and in clean and appropriate housing? If the lighting is poor and/or the smell is very bad, this is not a good store to patronize.

After making these observations, ask the staff a few questions about how they are caring for the iguanas. Ask about the diet they are feeding them, the temperature of the enclosure, how big iguanas will grow, and anything else you can think of. If the staff gives you incorrect answers or doesn't know the answers, you should purchase your iguana from a more knowledgeable source.

If the staff seems to know what they are talking about, the enclosures for the iguanas and other animals are appropriate for their denizens, and the majority of the animals appear alert and healthy, you have probably found a good store from which to purchase your iguana. When you were questioning the staff, if they recommended that you purchase a book on iguana care, this is a good sign that they care about their animals and try to see their animals go to good homes.

Pet shops are often the best places to pick your very own green iguana.

Once you find a good pet store, patronize it and develop a relationship with the owner or staff. Good pet stores can be terrific resources for keepers of iguanas, and if you are a regular customer, you may find it easier to get advice, special order any equipment you might need, or be shown new products and books that might be useful to you.

Adoption

Each year, hundreds of thousands of iguanas are purchased by all types of people across the US. In many cases, the buyer did not do the proper research on the keeping of these animals or carefully consider what having a large, tropical lizard as a pet would be like. Most of these iguanas will die. However, some survive until the owner decides to get rid of them. They might put a classified ad in the paper advertising an iguana for adoption, put up flyers at pet stores and veterinary offices, or drop the iguana off at a local animal shelter. Some particularly unthinking people will let their iguana go, almost assuredly sentencing their animal to misery and an unpleasant death. If the iguana is lucky, his owner will turn him over to a herp society that has an adoption service. Any of these places could be a source for you to acquire a "pre-owned" iguana.

Before adopting an iguana, there are some things you should consider. First of all, the iguana may not be in the best of health. Depending on why it was put up for adoption, the iguana could very well be suffering from neglect, malnutrition, or illness. You will have to decide if you have the resources to nurse such an animal back to health. Second, if the iguana was neglected, it is probably not socialized to people. If it is very young, you should be able to tame the animal and make it a nice pet. If the animal is an adult, attempts at taming may be less than successful.

As an example, several years ago I moved into a house that a friend of mine was vacating. He and his wife—after discussing this with me—left their iguana behind. This iguana, Petey, was a big male, probably four or five years old, who lived on a loft above the living room. He was never handled and had had one or two owners previous to my friend and his wife. Petey was aggressive and nasty. Attempts at handling or retraining him inevitably resulted in my being whipped and/or scratched. The only thing that saved Petey from finding yet another owner was that he and my female iguana, Kermit, got along like best friends. I still have both Petey and Kermit. Even after all these years of care and attempts at socializing, Petey is still unpredictable and not handleable. He has calmed somewhat, but he is not what most people would consider a nice pet. Adopting an unsocialized, adult iguana should be done without the expectation that this animal will become a tame pet.

If possible, adopting from a herp society is your best bet. Even if the original owner provided inadequate care, the staff of the herp society will have been keeping the iguana well for the time they've had it. They will also be able to tell you of any problems the iguana has and offer some informed advice on ways to remedy them. They also may have provided vet care or at least will recommend a veterinarian familiar with iguanas. Adopting from a herp society often requires a small donation, but don't let this deter you. Know that your money is going to help provide caring foster homes for unwanted iguanas and other reptiles and amphibians.

Adopting an iguana from an animal shelter or private person is more risky. Regular animal shelters do their best, but usually they do not have the resources or expertise to properly care for iguanas. Some of them actually have arrangements with herp societies or private individuals who love reptiles and place iguanas with one of these foster homes. If you are adopting an iguana from a regular cat-and-dog shelter, just be prepared for the lizard to be in rough shape. Depending on why the owner is getting rid of his or her iguana, the lizard may be in great shape or at death's door, may be tame or an unholy terror. Find out beforehand what the situation is and make sure you are prepared for the iguana you are receiving. If possible, visit the iguana before making up your mind as to whether or not this is the iguana you want to take home. Be realistic about your ability to care for an ill or aggressive iguana, or you may end up having to put him up for adoption yourself, which is hardly fair to the iguana.

Picking Out a Healthy Iguana

Now that you know about the various places you can go to buy an iguana, you should learn how to pick an iguana that's healthy and likely to make a good pet. Although you can never be 100 percent certain an iguana you'd like to purchase is in the best of health, there are several things you can do to help increase the chances that this is so. If you are buying your iguana from a pet store, you've already gotten a good start on finding a healthy iguana by shopping around and avoiding pet stores that are ignorant of proper iguana care. Although the circumstances when adopting an iguana will be different depending on the source of the adoption, this section will still help you in evaluating the health of the adoptee.

Most of the time, the iguanas in pet stores are babies. A baby will be less than 20 inches, nose to tail tip. You want an iguana that is this young to ensure that it starts its life as your pet with the proper care and socialization. It becomes increasing difficult to socialize iguanas as they get older, so start off with the youngest one you can.

Look over the group of iguanas for general healthy appearance. You want one with bright, alert eyes, not eyes that are half or fully closed. Sunken eyes are a definite sign of poor health. Observe how the iguana moves. It should not favor any of its limbs. It should have good color—generally a bright green with some brown banding, but the coloration is variable.

When picking out a new green iguana as a pet, be sure to examine it closely for any sign of diseases.

Once you have done this type of general inspection, you need to pick up the iguana for a closer inspection. This is a good time to get an idea of his temperament. Sometimes a baby iguana will come right over to you. This is rare (especially in pet stores; it is more likely if you are buying from a breeder), but it is a good sign that this iguana will be a friendly pet. Most likely, the iguana will run away. This is normal and not a cause for alarm. However, if the running is excessive and the lizard batters itself nearly senseless on the glass of the tank, this iguana might be a nervous one that will take some work to calm down. If he stands his ground, puffs up, hisses, and whips his tail, you may want to consider a less aggressive individual. These hostile iguanas do take some work to socialize, although since he is a baby, you still have a decent chance of taming him down.

Now that you have the iguana in hand, he will probably squirm a little and may open his mouth to bite. This is pretty normal. If he does open his mouth to bite, take this as an opportunity to look at the mouth lining. If there are sores, missing teeth, or a cheesy paste (this is reptile pus), that iguana has some health problems, and you should pick another one. The same is true if he seems to have no strength in his limbs.

The iguana should have good body weight. If it is light as a feather, you want to select a different one. When you turn it over, it should have no feces or other material smeared or

Iguanas to Avoid

Here's a quick list of some qualities to avoid when selecting an iguana.

Do not buy animals that:

Are listless, weak, and sitting with their eyes closed;

Have feces or other crust around the vent;

Are thin (with visible hipbones or backbones);

Have obvious sores, wounds, injuries, or broken limbs;

Have thickened or deformed jaws or thighs (signs of metabolic bone disease);

Have runny or crusty eyes, mouths, or nostrils (salt crust on nostrils is okay);

Whip, bite, and hiss when you attempt to handle them, though some running away and squirming are normal.

crusted around the vent. There should be no discharges from the nose or eyes, although it is possible there will be a bit of salt crusted on the nostrils; that should not cause alarm. The eyes should not be swollen or sunken. When you look at the base of the tail of an iguana, it should be rather oval, not indented at the sides. Visible outlines of hipbones or the backbone are signs of starvation or inadequate nutrition. It is important to know that iguanas that have metabolic bone disease may have very fat thighs that could appear healthy to the untrained eye. If the iguana's thighs look too fat, *gently* squeeze a thigh between your thumb and forefinger. If metabolic bone disease is present, the thigh will be rather hard, not like soft muscle tissue. Also, this disease often causes swelling and deformity of the jaws. I mention these points because metabolic bone disease is a very common disease of young iguanas.

If you follow this advice and the iguana you picked passes muster, you can be reasonably sure that you have started with a healthy pet. Now the little lizard is depending on you to keep him happy and healthy.

Homecoming

Once you have picked out and paid for your iguana, you should try to get it home and into its enclosure as soon as possible. Depending on the weather, there are various preparations you must make for the journey home.

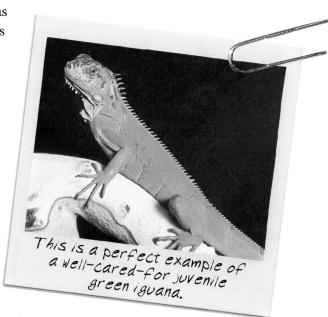

This is a perfect example of a well-cared-for juvenile green iguana.

The pet store, breeder, or expo vendor will put your iguana in either a box or a cloth sack. If the weather is mild (60°F or above), you need not worry about insulating your iguana, particularly if it is a short drive. If the drive is long and the temperature below 70°F, you should run the heater in the car. This will keep your iguana from getting too cold on the way home.

If the weather will be colder than 60°F or so, you will have to make slightly more elaborate preparations. Find a small, insulated container. This can be a Styrofoam box (like the ones in which fish and reptiles are shipped) or a small cooler. Place a towel

Iguana Sources

These are in order of preference, defined as which source is most likely to have healthy iguanas and knowledgeable staff:

1) Private breeder;

2) Reptile adoption service;

3) Herp expo;

4) Pet store;

5) Adoption through former owner or animal shelter.

or newspaper in the bottom. Keep this container indoors near a heater (not on the heating grate, just close) for a couple of hours before going to get the iguana. When you go into the store, bring it with you, and put the iguana inside, either loose (if you can ensure he won't get out) or inside a cloth bag or pillowcase. While you are in the store, leave the car running with the heat on. Once you leave the store, go to your car immediately, minimizing the time your boxed iguana is exposed to the harsh conditions.

No matter the weather, you should leave the pet store and head home immediately. The longer your iguana is not in adequate conditions, the more stressed he will be. Also, you don't want to leave him in the car while you run other errands. The car could become too hot or too cold in your absence, and your iguana could be severely distressed or worse by the time you return.

When you get home, immediately unpack your iguana and place him in his new home. The cage should be set up with the proper heating and lighting already waiting for the new arrival. Do not be surprised if your new pet is nervous and hides for the first day or two. The new surroundings are liable to stress him out. Also, although you should offer food, he may not eat for a day or two, especially if you are offering different food than he is used to. This should not cause alarm. If you are providing the correct housing, your iguana should begin to act normal in three days or less.

Refrain from handling him until he adapts to the new home. During this time, disturb him only for necessary cleaning and feeding. Try to observe the iguana carefully and unobtrusively as much as you can. It is best to catch any signs of disease early on. Early detection and prompt vet care will give your iguana the best chance of getting well.

Part Two
Understanding the Basics

"I know the fishbowl is cheap, but I get the feeling that the realtor wasn't telling us everything"

An Iguana's Cage is His Castle

Properly Housing Your Iguana

The enclosure you select for your iguana will play a large part in how well the lizard does under your care. Therefore, proper housing is critical in the successful keeping of iguanas (or any other reptile, for that matter). While there is nothing wrong with saving money, skimping on aspects of housing to save a few dollars could compromise your ig's health and safety–it's definitely not worth it. There are ways to save money when buying or making your iguana's cage, and we'll talk about some of those, but this chapter is mostly about housing your iguana the right way, not the cheap way.

Iguanas need spacious enclosures in order to thrive in captivity.

Care Checklist

When you first get your iguana, you might feel a bit overwhelmed by all the things you have to remember to do. Here is a quick list of what you have to do daily and weekly. Once you become more familiar with iguana care, you will be able to remember all of this on your own.

Typical Scenario

Here is one account of what happens when you buy the supplies for a baby iguana at most pet stores.

You enter the pet store and tell a salesperson you are buying an iguana soon and have come to buy the cage and accessories. The clerk shows you to the fish tanks and picks out a 10- or 20-gallon tank and screen top. If the person is at all knowledgeable, they also show you to the dome lights and suggest some heat bulbs. If not, they show you to the heat rocks and tell you that this is all the heat your iguana needs. Then you are sold some type of shredded bark for the bottom of the cage, a water bowl, and maybe a cave or piece of driftwood.

Once you get these materials together and set up, you go get your iguana. You immediately notice that he is almost as long as the length of the cage, if not longer. With otherwise proper care, your iguana grows rapidly. In about three months, your iguana can barely turn around in the cage. It seems he is always walking through his waste and upsetting the water bowl. He also spends nearly all of his time clutched to the heat rock, only moving off of it to eat.

If you have skipped ahead and read other sections of this book, you know there are several things wrong with this scenario. The cage must be bigger, heat has to come from above, there needs to be a source of ultraviolet light, and substrates must be carefully chosen. You can buy much of what you need for your iguana in a pet store, but you have to make those purchases armed with information on what your iguana needs and how you want to provide those needs. Let's start with the enclosure itself.

The Enclosure

There are a number of cage styles you can use to house your iguana. At least with a juvenile, the glass aquarium is the most popular choice. Adult iguanas are normally housed in custom-built cages, which can be made from any number of materials. Of course, there are other choices for housing your ig. Here we'll discuss the different types of enclosures and the advantages and drawbacks of each.

Glass Aquaria

Most often, people keep iguanas in fish tanks. There are several reasons for this, such as that they are relatively affordable, easily available, easy to clean, and visually appealing. Additionally, they are decent at holding heat and humidity. Probably the biggest reason people keep iguanas in aquaria is because that's what other people do! Aquaria do make a reasonable home for baby iguanas, but the aquarium big enough for a full-grown adult iguana would be prohibitively expensive, heavy, and difficult to clean. Another drawback to using aquaria is their fragility. It doesn't take much to crack one while cleaning it, and if you drop your fish tank or knock it over, you'll have to buy a new one immediately and clean up all the glass.

If you decide to start out with a fish tank, buy the biggest one you can afford. This gives you the longest time possible before you have to buy or build a bigger cage. I would recommend that you start with nothing smaller than a 30-gallon, and a 55- or 75-gallon would be a far better choice. A healthy and well-fed iguana can be expected to outgrow a 30-gallon in about a year; you may get two years out of a 75-gallon. Using an aquarium for any iguana over two years old is not recommended because of the size of the aquarium that would be needed—assuming you could find one that big.

Salt Removal

The best cleanser I've found for removing the salt iguanas secrete out of their nostrils is white vinegar. It is cheap, completely safe, and very effective. You can cut it with water if you like or use it straight. It may not smell nice, but it cleans up the salt deposits very quickly. I dab some on a rag and lightly scrub the deposits. They disappear quickly. I follow this up with a rinse, mostly to remove the odor.

Plastic Reptile Cages

In the herp hobby, there are a few brands of plastic cages that have sliding front doors. They are lightweight, easy to clean, good at holding heat and humidity, and look nice in the home. These are highly recommended for many lizards and snakes, but they are of limited use for iguanas. Most are not tall enough to satisfy an iguana's need to climb, nor are they made in sizes large enough for an adult iguana. They are also expensive, so if there were one big enough for a large iguana, it would probably be too costly for the average keeper to buy. If you want to use one for your baby iguana, it would not be a bad choice.

Commercial Screen Cages

Within the last five years, a few pet companies have marketed durable screen cages for the keeping of iguanas and chameleons. They are tall, sturdy, well ventilated, and not too heavy to lift and move. As with most commercially available housing options, they simply

Part 2

Iguanas will perch almost anywhere.

are not big enough to house adult iguanas. However, these cages are large enough for an iguana up to about three years of age, depending on the individual. The drawbacks to this type of cage are that, because it is made of wire, keeping the cage warm and humid enough for your ig can be a real challenge. Also, the wire mesh is large enough to possibly allow baby iguanas to escape. I've also found that cleaning these cages is more of a chore than the manufacturers would have you believe.

Spare Room

Some keepers allow their adult iguanas to have the run of a spare room or walk-in closet. Of course, the room must be properly outfitted with lights, heaters, humidifiers, climbing surfaces, and other necessary items. While this may seem like an extreme option, it provides your iguana with unparalleled space and the opportunity to choose exactly the temperature and humidity level he'd like at any given time. Because you can walk into the enclosure, cleaning it is not as much of a hassle as you might think.

The problems with this approach are having the space in your home to devote to an iguana and the strong chance that if you do not properly secure the lights and other fixtures, your iguana could injure itself or even others. As an illustration of this, I'll tell you about the time my iguanas lived in a loft. There was a loft above the living room that I had outfitted to house my pair of iguanas. I did not realize they could reach the heat lamps. When I was out, apparently one of the iguanas decided to climb on the lamp, which detached from its mounting and landed—still lit—on the linoleum floor of the loft. When I got home, the downstairs was full of evil-smelling smoke. Both the iguanas and the other pets were fine, and the only real damage done was a burn mark on the floor. However, had I stayed out for much longer, the house might have been on fire when I returned. So, if you choose to devote a room to your iguana, consider safety issues very carefully.

Custom-Built Cages

Most keepers eventually turn to building their own cage for their green friend. Indeed, this may be the best way to ensure that your enclosure meets all of your iguana's needs. There are a number of materials you could use to build the cage, and the furnishings are limited only by your iguana's needs and your imagination. A simple, custom-made cage can be built even by those who are less than handy. I know because I built my iguana cage with my stepfather, and I can barely tell which end of a screwdriver to use! Ideas for building your own cage will be covered later.

The major drawbacks to building your own cage are the time required to do so and having the proper tools and know-how. The advantages are that a custom-made cage costs a fraction of what the same cage would cost if you purchased it. Additionally, a custom cage perfectly fits into your space and décor, and you know that it provides all the proper housing parameters for your ig.

If you do not think you can build your own cage or want a custom cage but don't want to build it yourself, there are ways to have one built for you. At herp shows and in herp publications, you can find companies and individuals who make custom cages for housing reptiles. While these cages are not cheap, they are generally of excellent quality and make beautiful additions to your home. Also, because you are dealing with someone who likes reptiles, they are likely to have good insight into an iguana's needs and have some interesting stories to tell. Local carpenters are also a good source for custom-made cages.

Custom-built cages can provide much more space compared to manufactured types.

Along with custom-made enclosures, keepers have made use of a wide variety of alternative cages. With some modification, there are ways to make suitable housing out of greenhouses, cattle feeding troughs (for juveniles), shower stalls, television consoles (for juveniles), and other items limited only by human ingenuity. If you wish to try some novel approach to housing, keep your iguana's safety and needs at the forefront of your mind and you won't go far wrong.

Free Range

Some iguana keepers allow their iguanas to roam around their house or a large portion of it. They say it gives the iguana plenty of room and he becomes very tame and social. According to these keepers, it's more like having a real pet (i.e., a dog or a cat) than if the iguana were cooped up in a cage.

While this might sound appealing, there are a number of things to consider before you choose this housing option. First of all, the average household poses many dangers for your beloved ig. There are electrical cords that can tangle him up (possibly strangle him) or shock him if he bites them. There are heavy things that could be knocked over and glass items that can be broken. There may be small spaces that can be squeezed into but not squeezed out of. Houseplants and cleaning products are potential iguana poisons. Other pets in the home could decide your ig is an enemy or a meal. A door left carelessly open or a window with a weak screen means your iguana will escape, encountering all the dangers of the outside world. The list goes on.

Some owners allow their green iguanas to roam freely around the house.

Aside from the dangers to your pet, there are the dangers to your family and your possessions. If an iguana knocks over a lamp, there could be a fire. Any fragile knick-knacks are likely to be destroyed eventually. If your iguana crawls into the kitchen and over the food preparation areas, the entire family may be infected with salmonella. If your iguana is less than perfectly potty trained, expect your rugs, sofas, chairs, and such to become stained or completely ruined.

Finally, even if these hazards are prevented, you must also be sure that your iguana has access to the proper heating, lighting, humidity, and food. The environment your iguana needs is much easier to provide in an enclosure than in a whole house or apartment. Especially at first, your iguana may just not realize where his basking perches are and not be able to get back to them when he cools off.

If you are bound and determined to give your iguana the run of several rooms, there are several things you can do to help make the situation safe for him, your family, and your stuff. Remove all the possible dangers: houseplants, knick-knacks, electrical cords, flimsy screens, loose and broken duct grates, and *anything else you can think of.* Remember, if an iguana can possibly injure itself or cause damage with some item, it probably will. You have to become an expert trouble-shooter if you plan on letting your iguana roam all the time.

You also have to set up areas for your iguana to bask, feed, and eliminate. Shelves with lights suspended over them work well. You'll need to prop up a large limb or other iguana ladder so that your ig can get up to his basking shelves. A sturdy board that has natural-fiber rope or twine attached horizontally across the surface works for this purpose.

Green iguanas that have free range often frequent their cages several times during the day.

When free-ranging your iguana, keep his food and water bowls in the same place. If you move them, he will not always be able to find them when he's hungry or thirsty.

Because iguanas generally like to defecate in one spot, it's relatively easy to keep your ig from soiling furnishings. Find the spot your iguana has picked as his toilet and put a low-sided cat litter pan there. It can be filled with aspen shavings, shredded newspaper, paper towels, recycled newspaper animal bedding, or even left empty. Just do not use kitty litter, as this material can cause intestinal blockages if your iguana swallows some. Each day, you'll need to clean out the pan after your iguana uses it. Once your iguana has an adequate spot, he will rarely choose to go elsewhere. Since iguanas tend to go when they are in the water, you can get your ig to eliminate on your schedule by putting him in a basin of room temperature water once a day.

Size: It Matters

Most folks buy iguanas as babies, when they are no more than 10 to 15 inches in total length. It's difficult to conceive of that little green sprout growing into a 5-foot giant. It's even more difficult to conceive of how fast this growth takes place. You can reasonably

The size of the cage is very important to the green iguana's overall health.

Housing at a Glance

When buying or building your iguana enclosure, here's a quick list of what an iguana habitat needs to provide.

Space: iguanas grow large and like to have room.

Height: iguanas like to climb.

Light: light provides your iguana with a day/night cycle, allows him to utilize calcium, and can help food look more appealing.

Heat: iguanas should be able to warm their bodies up to about 100°F through basking.

Humidity: iguanas prefer relative humidity around 80 percent.

Ventilation: heat + humidity + no air movement = mold, bacteria, and other pathogens.

Safety: the enclosure and everything inside must be sturdy and safe for your iguana.

expect your iguana to double in size before the end of the first year you have him and to triple in size before the end of the second year. This presents a number of housing challenges. The enclosure that is ideal for your iguana initially will be far too small within 15 months. Conversely, if you start with a cage of the proper size for an adult iguana, a baby could get lost in all that space (and probably never get used to handling; he'll just run and hide when you enter the cage).

Given their size, iguanas like to have a lot of space to move around in. Remember that these are animals at home in the trees; they like to climb. When designing or buying a cage, you have to provide them with plenty of space in all directions.

When I talk to people about housing iguanas and other reptiles, they always seem to want to know what would be the smallest cage in which they can house their pet. To me, this seems to be a rather poor way of starting out with a pet. It would be better to think about what kind of space the animal needs in order to be happy or at least comfortable.

The minimum size of an enclosure I recommend for iguanas is probably larger than you may have seen in other books, been told by the pet store, or seen on the Internet. However, I firmly believe that the more space you can give your iguana (within reason; a baby certainly won't be happy or safe if given an extra bedroom all to himself), the better off the iguana will be.

Keeping that in mind, I recommend housing an iguana in a cage that is 1.5 times as long as he is, at least half as deep as he is long, and at least as tall as he is long. I would never keep an iguana in anything smaller for the long term. Ideally, your iguana will be in a cage that is larger than the dimensions given here.

Heating and Lighting

These two factors of iguana housing are critically important ones. I devote a separate, small section on lighting because of its importance and the complexity of the different types of light available. Here we will just talk about the temperature and light needs of an iguana. In a later section, we will talk about how to meet the temperature and lighting needs of your iguana.

Enclosures housing green iguanas should be outfitted with plenty of branches and shelves for climbing and exercise.

Back in the section on the biology and anatomy of iguanas, you may remember that I said that iguanas get their heat from the sun. Sunlight also provides the ultraviolet light they need to make vitamin D3, the reptilian version of vitamin D. What this means for you when you are designing your ig's cage is that you have to provide heat that comes from above. You also should have the heat and the light coming from close to the same place. If you put all the lights at one end of the cage and the heat at the other, your iguana may become confused, spending all of his time under the light but never getting warm enough to digest his food, or spending all of his time under the heat and not getting the ultraviolet light he needs. Keeping the heat and light near each other simulates the natural environment your iguana is adapted to.

Lighting for the Free-Ranging Iguana

If you let your iguana roam and set him up a nice, brightly lit area for heating and basking, you may find he prefers the sunlit window. Iguanas almost always prefer sunlight to any kind of artificial light. At first you may think this is fine. However, window glass screens out ultraviolet light. Your ig will be getting the heat he needs but not the ultraviolet light. Windowscreens do not stop UV light, but they could lead to drafts. It might be possible to replace part of the preferred basking window with UV-transparent glass or plastic panes that let most of the UV through.

To make sure your enclosure is the proper temperature, you need to invest in a thermometer or, ideally, more than one. You'll want to know the temperature at the warmest part of the cage and at the coolest. You'll also want to know how high and how low the temperature gets at these spots throughout the day. For that reason, the best thermometers to use are the digital ones that store the highest and lowest temperatures reached each day (mini-max). These can be purchased at most electronics stores. They range widely in price and the more expensive models have more bells and whistles, but all you really need is a thermometer that stores the highs and lows. You'll need one for the warmest spot of the cage and one for the coolest.

Avoid the plastic strip thermometers that stick on the side of the cage. They are inaccurate and can lead to you keeping your iguana much cooler or much warmer than is healthy for him. Back when I did use this type of thermometer, I also found they stopped working after about 18 months or so.

Iguanas do best when the air temperature in their enclosure is in the low 80s. There should be a hot spot that reaches 95° to 100°F. To accommodate your iguana's natural behaviors, the hot spot should be up near the top of the enclosure and should be created by heat coming from above. The hot spot should also be large enough for your iguana to fit his entire body in comfortably. It does little good if the iguana has to choose to heat his belly, his head, or some other part while leaving the rest of his body cool.

At night, your iguana should have a small drop in temperature, but nighttime temperatures in the cage should be no lower than 75°F. If temperatures in your house get lower than this at night–and in most houses they do–you will need to use some form of heating for your iguana at night.

Iguanas can tolerate temperatures outside of these values, but such temperatures cause the lizard stress. Prolonged exposure to extreme temperatures will cause injury and eventually death. Iguanas do not tolerate temperatures below 50°F very well, and even brief exposures to such temperatures can cause serious problems. Iguanas suffer heat stroke and death at roughly 115°F if they cannot get out of such heat.

How to Heat Your Iguana

Although your iguana has a small range of temperatures he will do best at, there are a few different ways to meet his temperature needs. Which option or options you choose is up to you; so long as the iguana's needs are met, the methods used are not critical. Most iguana keepers use a mix of heat sources to be sure that their iguanas are comfortable and healthy.

Heat Lamps

Using high-wattage bulbs to generate heat in an iguana's cage is probably the most popular option with keepers. It is the most obvious method and one of the more cost-effective. Also, the materials are not difficult to obtain.

If you choose this method, be sure you do not use bulb wattages that are too high or too low. Avoid this problem by using accurate thermometers and by checking the temperature at various times of the day. Remember to keep tabs on the temperature as the seasons change. You will probably need to use lower-wattage bulbs in the summer and higher-wattage bulbs in the winter. Another way to change the temperature inside the cage is to move the lights closer or farther away from the cage.

When using heat lamps, it is best if you use fixtures that have ceramic sockets. These are the most durable and are the type best able to withstand the amount of heat being generated, especially if you are using very high-wattage bulbs (over 150 watts). You really do not need any special type of light bulb to heat the enclosure. All incandescent lights generate substantial amounts of heat, so the regular bulbs you use for the lamps in your home will work fine. Just make sure the temperature is correct, and the type of bulb will not matter.

To make the hot spot large enough for the iguana, you may have to use more than one lamp. Put them next to each other to create a hot spot that your iguana can fit under comfortably. I use two heat lamps and a ceramic heat emitter (see below) all next to each

As-needed Care

Remove and replace entire substrate.

Dump, disinfect, and refill litter pan.

Wipe dirt and dust off the lights.

Clean the outside of the enclosure: wipe down the glass, dust off the wire, etc.

Clean under the enclosure (at least once a month).

Clean and disinfect the humidifier (at least once a month; twice a month is best).

other to generate a hot spot large enough for Petey to fit his entire body.

Over the years, heat lamps have been the death of many iguanas. Others now bear permanent scars because of heat lamps. You have to be completely sure that your heat lamp and your iguana never come into contact. I have my heat lamps suspended a few inches above my cage by some rope (being careful, of course, that the rope cannot be burned by the lamps). Although the mesh under the lamps gets very hot, it does not get hot enough to cause serious burns. Even given the danger of burns, heat lamps are a good method for heating your iguana. If you are careful, the danger posed by heat lamps can be negated.

Ceramic Heat Emitters

These are essentially lightbulbs that generate heat without generating any light. Although you must be cautious when using them, I find them to be a wonderful heat source for iguanas and many other reptiles.

The fact that these items do not generate light makes them ideal for heating the enclosure at night. A glaring heat lamp would disturb your pet's natural sleep cycle (and may disturb your own if the cage is in or near your bedroom), but heat emitters just provide warmth.

Ceramic heat emitters put out a lot of heat. You cannot safely use them in a regular light fixture; the fixture would melt and possibly catch on fire. You have to buy a ceramic light fixture. Because of the amount of heat put out by these emitters, you must be very careful that they cannot burn your iguana and that they are not near curtains, paper, or other flammable substances.

You can buy heat emitters and the proper fixtures for them at pet stores that carry lots of reptiles, herp shows, and online herp supply companies. They are expensive, but the manufacturers guarantee them for three to five years. I have one that is going on seven years old. So, although it seems like a lot of money to spend for a specialized lightbulb, you won't have to replace the emitter for at least three years, barring some type of accident.

Ceramic Heat Panels

These are square or rectangular panels that emit heat. You can think of them as a ceramic heat emitter made into a flat square. They are manufactured for use with reptiles and baby birds. They haven't really caught on in the herp hobby, but they are a useful product for heating cages.

Generally, heat panels are mounted on the side of a cage, creating a warmer end. To use these with iguanas, you could mount one high up in the cage and then position a branch directly in front of it.

I've never seen these for sale other than at herp shows. They should also be available through online herp suppliers, and your local pet store may be able to special order them for you. All of the precautions you would use with the ceramic heat emitters apply to this product. Follow the manufacturer's instructions for usage to the letter.

Pig Blankets

These are essentially large heating pads that are marketed for use with baby pigs and other mammals. The reptile hobby has caught on to the usefulness of these items for heating large enclosures.

These put out a good amount of heat, but because they are made specifically to put baby animals directly on them, they do not get hot enough to cause burns. They are very useful for heating the floor of an iguana cage. However, they may be hard to use to create a hot spot. It may be possible to get one the size of your iguana's perch and secure it to that. If I were housing my iguanas in a room, I would certainly include a shelf with one of these on it.

Because they are used for baby mammals, pig blankets are durable and easily cleaned. Some come with thermostats built in so that you can select the temperature you want the blanket to generate. If I were to buy one, I would certainly buy one that has an adjustable thermostat.

You can get pig blankets at farm-supply stores, herp shows, and from advertisers in reptile publications. Pig blankets can be expensive, but they are a good choice of a heat source.

Human Heating Pads

These are much the same as a pig blanket, but they are generally smaller and made for human use. They can be used in much the same way as a pig blanket.

Human heating pads need to be continually monitored for temperature. For some reason, I've found they fluctuate quite a bit. Maybe the manufacturers figure that the user will just remove it or turn the heat down if it gets uncomfortable. However, iguanas cannot do this. You need to keep tabs on how hot are the pad and your iguana.

These heating devices are excellent for times when you have your iguana out of his cage for any length of time or for use in emergencies. They are less useful as a heat source within the cage.

Hot Rocks are Bad!

Many pet stores that are inexperienced with reptiles recommend electrically heated artificial rocks (usually called hot rocks or heat rocks) for use with iguanas. There are many reasons why these are not just unnecessary but dangerous for iguanas.

The rocks go on the bottom of the cage; your iguana likes to stay at the top.

The rocks only heat a small spot of the cage, not the air.

Over time, these rocks sometimes develop spots that are much hotter than they should be, creating a risk of serious burns.

If you use one as your main source of heat, your iguana will sit on the rock all the time, which will eventually cause burns.

Because of these reasons, hot rocks are a bad idea to include in the cage of most reptiles and are certainly dangerous for iguanas. Do not use them.

Undertank Heaters

You can think of these heating items as smaller versions of pig blankets. They are designed for use with reptiles by a number of manufacturers. They have an adhesive side that sticks to the bottom of a glass fish tank. When plugged in, they generate a temperature in the neighborhood of 100°F (varies by type and manufacturer).

Because of the method of using undertank heaters, they are of limited use for heating iguanas. They can be used for juveniles kept in glass aquaria to heat the bottom. I've heard of keepers attaching them to the wall of an aquarium, but having no experience with this method, I can't be sure the results were satisfactory.

You can buy undertank heaters in almost any pet store that carries reptiles. You can also try herp shows and online herp suppliers.

Heat Tape and Similar Items

Heat tape comes in a thin, rolled sheet and when plugged in generates heat. It is usually rolled out across a shelf and taped or tacked down. Cages are then put on top of it. Similar devices called heat strips and heat cables are also available. Many of these products originally were developed to keep pipes from freezing, but now there are brands manufactured specifically for use with herps.

Like undertank heaters, the method of using heat tape limits its use as an iguana-heating device. I do know someone who heated his frilled dragons (which climb and bask much like an iguana) by running heat tape through a hollow branch to create a hot spot. With some ingenuity, you could find a way to make heat tape work for your iguana, but it would probably not replace other forms of heating.

Heat tape is available at herp shows, from advertisements in reptile publications, and from online herp suppliers.

Thermostats

Although thermostats do not in themselves generate heat, they help to regulate the temperature within your ig's enclosure. They shut off heating devices when the cage gets too hot and turn the heat on when the cage gets too cool.

I highly recommend the use of a thermostat. They can prevent many problems related to your iguana getting too hot or too cool. They are fully worth the price. Be sure the thermostat you buy can handle the wattage of the heating devices you run through it.

Advanced thermostats come with internal timers. This allows you to set different temperatures for different times of the day (a night temperature and a day temperature). This is a very useful feature, but it is not necessary.

There are thermostats manufactured specifically for use with herps. They can be purchased at herp shows, through the ads in herp publications, and through online herp suppliers. You can buy regular thermostats at most hardware stores and at electronics stores.

Humidity

When you build your ig's new home, you have to account for how much humidity in the air your iguana wants and needs. This is a critical area of iguana husbandry that is frequently overlooked by many keepers.

Easy Disinfection

When you own an iguana or other pets, having a safe, effective, and inexpensive disinfectant comes in handy. One that fits this description is a solution of bleach and water.

You can buy a handheld plant-misting bottle at most supermarkets, department stores, or garden centers. Clearly label it as containing bleach to avoid any accidents. Most of these misters have a guide on them telling you how to make solutions of various concentrations. You want to make a solution of 20 percent bleach and 80 percent water.

Once you have the solution, you can spray it on any soiled surface. (Note that this will stain fabrics; basically take any of the precautions you normally would when using bleach.) Let the spray sit on the surface for at least 15 minutes. After this, wipe it up and rinse the surface.

While this solution will not kill all pathogens, it is broadly effective and works against most of the germs carried by iguanas and other pets.

In the wild, iguanas tend to live in areas that have an average relative humidity of 80 percent or higher. In captivity, you need to supply your iguana with an average relative humidity of 70 percent to 90 percent. If you do not keep your iguana humid enough, he can develop a host of problems including difficulty shedding, skin irritations, respiratory infections, eye problems, and kidney and urinary problems.

There are several ways to keep a proper level of humidity in your iguana's enclosure. I've found that combining methods works best. Most electronics stores carry hygrometers, devices that measure the humidity in the air. This is a handy piece of equipment to have.

One of the most frequently used methods to raise humidity is the plant mister. You fill it with water and spray the iguana's cage. These are extremely useful devices for any keeper of reptiles to have. Generally, to keep the humidity in the proper range, you will need to spray your ig's cage at least twice a day. Avoid spraying the cage right before the lights go out. This causes the temperature to drop farther than it would otherwise and also seems to lead to respiratory problems, probably due to increases in bacterial populations.

Because of the size of an iguana's cage, a hand-held plant mister may not make a tremendous difference in the relative humidity. In this case, consider using a humidifier.

There are many types, but all efficiently put water into the air. Using one of these you can humidify a whole room. Warm air humidifiers may seem like the best choice, but you must be careful that your iguana cannot get into the steam, touch the humidifier, or knock it over. These humidifiers themselves get very hot and can cause severe burns, while the steam could scald an iguana that got too near it. Cold air humidifiers are safer, but I find they make things in the surrounding area very clammy–not that your iguana will mind. A more serious concern is that a cool air humidifier will make it difficult to keep the cage warm enough.

The best choice is the ultrasonic humidifier. This produces a vapor that is neither particularly warm nor particularly cold. It may be a little more expensive, but it is worth the difference in price. Humidifiers are available at most department stores and pharmacies.

Although mainly used in the keeping of chameleons and frogs, rainmakers can be adapted for use with iguanas. A rainmaker is like an automatic plant mister. It generally consists of a bucket that serves as a reservoir, a water pump, some hose, and one or more nozzles from which the water emerges in a fine mist. These are excellent devices for misting iguanas, but they create one problem: where does all that water go? With smaller cages you can arrange buckets or pans beneath the cages to catch the water, but at the size of an iguana cage this becomes impractical. Unlike chameleons that need nearly constant moving water, iguanas generally do not need the mister to come on more than once or twice a day. Depending on the conditions in your cage and in your home, this might not create a substantial amount of run-off. One solution to any run-off is fairly drastic: having the iguana cage in a room that includes a drain in the floor. I've also heard of keepers having their ig's enclosure inside of a kiddie pool that is periodically drained. The enterprising iguana keeper could come up with other, better solutions.

Older books on iguana care often stated that keeping a large water bowl in the cage would keep the humidity in the proper range. While a large water bowl contributes to the humidity, it alone does not do the job. Iguanas like a large water bowl, so you should provide one. Just don't expect it to maintain the humidity.

Some keepers keep the cage mostly enclosed because that makes it easier to keep the humidity in the acceptable range. However, that decreases ventilation, causing the air to become stale and still. This creates an ideal breeding ground for molds, fungi, bacteria, and other undesirables. If you notice mold growing in your iguana cage, you probably need to take steps to increase the ventilation and/or need to clean the cage more frequently.

Soaking

Iguanas will benefit from occasional soaks in the tub or shower. I recommend giving your iguana a good soak every week. The water temperature should be about the same temperature as the air. A soak should be at least a half-hour long, and an hour would do no harm.

Bathing your iguana will help keep the skin soft and make shedding less stressful.

To soak your iguana, you can fill a large plastic tub or your bathtub with enough water to submerge the iguana up to his elbows. This depth gives him enough water to soak in but not so much that he has to constantly swim to keep his head up. You must keep an eye on your ig even when the water is at the recommended depth. It would be unusual to have an iguana drown in such a low water level, but it is certainly possible. Iguanas can stay submerged for long periods of time, so try not to be alarmed if he's completely under for 10 minutes or so. Just check to see if he's all right without panicking.

Be aware that your iguana will probably eliminate in the water, so be prepared to change the water partway through the soaking time. I've sometimes had to change the water twice when soaking my igs.

I do not recommend putting your iguana in the shower with the water running. I've found that the temperature of the water coming out the showerhead can vary considerably over the duration of the shower. This is especially true if you live in an apartment; if someone on another floor flushes, your iguana may get scalded! I really am not joking about this. I nearly killed a bunch of frogs I was showering (in preparation for breeding) when the water temperature became extremely hot to the touch.

If you use the bathtub for soaking, be sure to disinfect it immediately afterward.

Lighting

While lighting and heating are often thought of together, they are separate housing parameters. Because light often provides heat, they are related, but they do serve different functions. In nature, light comes from the sun and provides an iguana with three things (probably more, but we can verify three): illumination (enabling the lizard to see and providing a sense of time), heat, and vitamin D. Yes, an iguana gets its vitamin D from the sunlight, not from the diet. The situation in the wild is such that iguanas bask to get warm and produce vitamin D in the process–more about this later. We already talked about the heating function of light, so this section will concentrate on the other two functions of light.

Like humans, iguanas are highly visual creatures, and also like humans, sight is probably their most important sense. The rhythms of light and dark tell your iguana that the days are passing, when to feed and mate, and when to take shelter for the night. Therefore, you must provide light for your iguana, and the lighting you use must perform the same three functions as sunlight: heating, illumination, and generation of vitamin D. The everyday lightbulbs you use at home only perform the first two functions. The latter function requires special lightbulbs that we'll be discussing shortly.

To provide a natural photoperiod, you turn the lights on in the morning and off in the evening. It is easiest to have the lights on timers. This provides your lizard with the same photoperiod every day without you having to remember when to turn lights on and off. You may want to vary the photoperiod with the seasons, providing longer days in the summer and shorter days in the winter. Varying the photoperiod is probably not necessary for normal keeping, but it is often crucial to success in the breeding of many species. By having a timer, you will find it easy to vary the photoperiod by just resetting the timer, rather than trying to remember to turn the lights off an hour earlier (and arranging to be home and available to do so).

Photoperiod

When talking about the cycle of day and night (or light and dark when discussing an animal caged indoors), you are talking about a photoperiod. A working definition of photoperiod would be, "the hours of light and dark during a 24-hour period." This is usually expressed as a ratio of the hours of light to the hours of darkness. If you have the lights on for 14 hours a day in your iguana enclosure, the photoperiod is 14:10. Photoperiod and its changes over the course of a year influence mating, feeding, sleeping, and other behaviors.

Your iguana should receive 12 to 14 hours of light per day. If you are not going to breed your iguana, you do not need to ever change the photoperiod.

The last function of light may be the most important for the iguana keeper to understand. In nature, sunlight provides iguanas and many other species of lizards with the vitamin D that they need. It is not just any light that will do this, but the part of sunlight known as ultraviolet B waves (UVB for short). Exposure to UVB activates an enzyme in a lizard's skin, which in turn transmutes a vitamin D precursor into vitamin D3 (it's actually much more complicated, but that will do for the purposes of keeping an iguana alive and healthy). Without such exposure, many species will be vitamin D deficient. Vitamin D3 is responsible for proper calcium metabolism, so lizards that are deficient have thin, weak bones, bone deformities, and muscle tremors. Because young lizards are growing rapidly, they will express these problems more quickly than adults.

How does an iguana kept indoors get UVB? There are several ways. Obviously, sunlight is the best source of UVB and other useful light wavelengths, so when possible it is always a good idea to expose your pet to natural sunlight. However, this is not possible for many keepers. Luckily, there are artificial lights that provide levels of UVB sufficient for your pet to remain in good health. Most of these are fluorescent bulbs that generate little heat, but recently an incandescent bulb that emits both heat and UVB has come onto the market and is being recommended by some professional lizard breeders.

Whenever possible, you should allow your green iguana full exposure to unfiltered sunlight.

There are some things to know about the fluorescent bulbs that generate UVB. First, buy one that specifically states both that it is for use with reptiles and that it emits UVB. There are some inferior brands on the market; if you stick with this recommendation, you will screen out most of those. Plant bulbs are not the same thing, and they do not generate significant amounts of UVB. Second, fluorescent bulbs will need to be replaced at least once a year (twice a year is better). They stop emitting UVB before they stop emitting light, so you will not know by looking at one when the bulb needs to be replaced. Here's a tip for you: write down the date your lightbulb needs to be replaced on a small sticker and place this directly on the light fixture. This will let you keep track of replacing the bulbs easily. Third, most of the bulbs must be within one foot of your pet for the iguana to receive any UVB. If you position the basking platform beneath the light, make sure it is within this suggested distance so the lizard may perch on the wood and soak up the ultraviolet (remember the warnings about iguanas getting too close to bulbs from the heating sections, however).

Within the past few years, new UVB-producing lightbulbs have come on the market. They are sold under the names Active UV Heat and Power-Sun. They are incandescent bulbs, so they screw right into a light fixture. There are three great things about them: they produce heat and UVB, eliminating the need for several bulbs; they produce more UVB than the fluorescent bulbs; and they produce a white light that makes colors appear very similar to the way they would under sunlight. Additionally, they can last up to five years. The drawback is that they are expensive. These bulbs also tend to be a bit fragile, especially when hot. Be careful not to jar one or get it wet if it's been on for a while. These bulbs should be about 18 inches from your lizard, as they produce a lot of heat and ultraviolet light. Because they get so hot, always use a ceramic fixture for one of these bulbs. Using a regular light socket can result in malfunction and a possible fire.

I've had nothing but good experiences with these bulbs, and I've used them on a number of different reptiles: chameleons, tortoises, bearded dragons, anoles, and, of course, iguanas. I can't recommend them highly enough.

One other type of bulb is sometimes used to provide UVB to iguanas and other lizards. These are mercury vapor bulbs. Like the incandescent UVB bulbs, they produce quite a lot of heat and UVB.

Last, most glass will absorb almost all the UVB. There should be no glass or plastic (unless stated to be UVB transparent) between your iguana and the light. Screen will allow UVB to pass freely.

Substrate

Often referred to as bedding, the substrate is the material you put on the floor of the cage. The major functions of a substrate are to absorb wastes and give your pet some traction as he moves around the cage. Depending on the substrate you choose, it may also help maintain the humidity in the enclosure, look nice, and help create a healthy environment.

The problem with discussing substrate is that there probably is no more controversial subject in the herp hobby. Each reptile keeper has a favorite substrate and can produce a list of why all other substrates are inferior or even dangerous. My goal is to attempt to keep the discussion of substrates grounded in reality and present the facts. However, I will be giving some recommendations.

The ideal substrate would be easy to clean, safe for the iguana, inexpensive, absorbent, and long lasting. It would also be esthetically pleasing and not have an unpleasant odor. You will probably find that with real substrates you must reach some form of compromise.

Aspen and Pine Shavings

Widely used for small animals, aspen and other wood shavings are used by some reptile keepers. While you could use this type of substrate for your iguana, it would be very problematic and possibly unsafe. These beddings get soggy and gross as soon as they get wet, which in a humid iguana enclosure would be in about three seconds. They also present a danger of impaction should your iguana swallow them.

> **Warning:**
> **Pine Kills**
>
> Pine-scented cleansers contain oils that are harmful to iguanas and other reptiles. Do not use these to clean your ig's cage or even to clean the room that has the enclosure in it. Also, avoid any cleansers that contain phenol, another potential iguana toxin.

If you really want to try this type of bedding, use aspen. Pine is less satisfactory, as it gets soggy very fast and may have oils that irritate your ig. *Never* use cedar shavings, because the oils are irritating and toxic to reptiles, amphibians, birds, and most small mammals. All in all, wood shavings are not recommended for iguanas.

Cypress Mulch

The shredded bark of cypress and similar trees is available at almost any good gardening store and at some hardware and department stores. In large quantities it is rather inexpensive. It doesn't smell bad and looks nice. Cypress mulch holds humidity rather well, helping to maintain the humidity in the air inside your ig enclosure. It does tend to need frequent cleaning, as soiled areas will get moldy fast. Some keepers claim this substrate causes gut impactions, but there is no solid data to confirm that it does so in iguanas.

Overall, this is one of the better substrates. It has its drawbacks, but it is safe and absorbent.

Newspaper, Paper Towels, and Similar Items

Whether you use newspaper, paper towels, cut-up paper bags, butcher paper, or some type of paper in sheets, the situation is the same. You have a cheap and easily cleaned substrate. The main drawback to using these materials as substrates is that they must be cleaned frequently. Whenever your iguana makes a mess (whether the mess is dumping the food bowl, sloshing water, or defecating), you must replace the substrate. This usually amounts to replacing the substrate–or part of it–every day to every other day.

Besides the price (often these substrates are free), the major advantage to using newspaper is safety. Sheets of paper pose no hazard to your ig. There is a small possibility that the bleaches used to make paper white can be harmful; use only newspaper or brown papers and you avoid this problem.

I use a combination of newspaper and brown paper bags in my iguana cage. It isn't pretty, but it works for me.

Potting Soil Mixes

Potting soil or some mix of potting soil and similar materials is often advocated by herpers seeking a "natural" material to use as a substrate. The trouble is that most potting soils are far from natural, being impregnated with chemical sterilizers and fertilizers and some form of aerator (perlite or pieces of Styrofoam). Potting soil mixes are generally only suitable for the naturalistic vivaria used to house small day geckos, anoles, treefrogs, and other tiny herps.

Because of the possible chemical and solid additives and a very real danger of causing gut impactions, I advise that you not use potting soil as a substrate for your iguana.

Rabbit Pellets

I've seen pelleted rabbit and guinea pig foods being used as a substrate for some iguanas and tortoises. The rationale here is that these herps are herbivorous, so keeping them on some edible plant-based bedding is good for them. This may not be the case.

Although the pellets smell good and can be eaten by the iguana, they pose several real problems when used as a substrate. They are extremely dusty, causing possible irritation to the eyes and respiratory system. When they get wet, they turn into a disgusting, clumpy,

Part 2

oatmeal-like material. This material quickly becomes laden with mold and bacteria. Because the pellets are edible and often very tasty to your iguana, he is very likely to eat the mold-ridden paste, which can cause illness or death. As if that weren't enough of a discouragement, this type of bedding is neither inexpensive nor very easy to clean. I don't recommend it.

Recycled Paper Bedding

This substrate is actually a by-product of the process used to recycle newsprint. It's sold under a few different names and looks like gray, thready lumps. It is soft to the touch and very absorbent. This substrate helps maintain humidity, but it is not overly prone to growth of molds and fungi. It has a strange odor that some people like and others detest.

Recycled paper bedding is lightweight, and it cleans up pretty easily. It's easy to spot-clean messes, allowing you to clean the whole substrate less often.

The big drawback of this substrate is the price. It is probably the most expensive of the substrates discussed here.

One of the best features of recycled paper bedding is that it passes harmlessly through the digestive tract of reptiles, eliminating any chance of impaction. As far as I am able to determine, this is the safest substrate next to newspaper. I use this substrate for nearly all of my herps and in my iguanas' litter pan.

Reptile Bark

A number of different companies market several different types of bark chips for use with reptiles. All of them are absorbent, fairly easy to clean and spot-clean, and resistant to mold. Reptile barks help with maintaining humidity.

Reptile barks do have a number of drawbacks, the first of which is the price. These are not cheap and are nearly as expensive as recycled paper bedding. Although they are sometimes advertised as dust-free, I've found most of these

Artificial Turf is Bad!

Once recommended frequently as a substrate for iguanas and other reptiles, artificial turf is now recognized as dangerous to these animals. As the turf ages, little bits break off. These create choking and impaction hazards. Loose strands have become wrapped around the toes of lizards, cutting off circulation and causing the toe to become gangrenous. The strands have also caused near asphyxiation of some iguanas. Lastly, it is nearly impossible to thoroughly clean artificial turf, leading to a buildup of bacteria and other pathogens.

Do not use artificial turf in your iguana's enclosure.

products to be fairly dusty. Lastly, there are many anecdotal reports of reptile barks causing impactions. I think these are an adequate choice for a substrate, but there are far better ones.

Reptile Carpeting

You may never have heard of such material, but reptile carpeting does exist. It is marketed as a safe substrate for use in reptile cages. It is rather safe. It also looks good, although certainly not natural. It absorbs wastes fairly well and can help maintain humidity.

This is expensive stuff. The packaging also says you can wash and reuse it. However, I've found it nearly impossible to get all of the wastes out of the material. This creates a health hazard for your iguana. I guess you could buy it and replace it every time you needed to, but that would become prohibitively expensive. If you can find a way to get all of the excretement out of it, it would be a great substrate.

Sand and Gravel

While these materials may be highly recommended for use in the housing of desert-dwelling lizards and snakes, they are not recommended for iguanas. They are dusty and do not absorb liquids very well. Additionally, when using these materials you are exposing your iguana to a very high risk of gut impaction. I discourage readers from using them for their iguanas.

Perches and Climbing Areas

Iguanas need to climb, and they are most comfortable if they can rest at least a few feet off of the ground. You must provide your iguana with suitable elevated resting areas and climbing surfaces that provide access to the resting areas.

Shelves

The best materials to use for perches are wooden shelves. The shelves should be about a foot wide, so your iguana can roost on them comfortably. They should be attached high up in the cage. Using multiple shelves at different levels is recommended.

Try to use a variety of materials for perches and shelves in your iguana's enclosure.

This gives your iguana the choice of how high up he wants to be, allowing him to select his body temperature based on how close to the heat lamp he wants to be. Be sure that one of the shelves is no more than 18 inches from the ultraviolet light.

Roosting shelves can also be made from melamine, which is a laminated pressboard material. It's sturdy and holds up well to cleaning and such. The lamination actually makes it quite a bit easier to clean than regular wood. Most well stocked building supply stores carry melamine shelving. It is more expensive than most wooden shelves.

Metal shelves are problematic to use. They may get too hot under the heat lamps, so you have to monitor the temperature. Additionally, with the humidity and the cleaning, they are liable to rust quickly. However, I know keepers who use metal shelves without a problem.

Branches and Limbs

To access the shelves, your iguana will need some type of ladder. There are a number of different items that will serve as iguana ladders. Large branches and limbs are probably the best so that your iguana can run from the floor of the cage up to the shelves. The best limbs and branches are those that are rough and bumpy, giving your iguana plenty of surfaces for traction. Smooth limbs make climbing difficult. If you end up with smooth limbs, you can use a saw to make small cuts in the wood, thus providing your ig with more grip. Another option would be to attach natural fiber rope around the branch every few inches. This will also give him more purchase and allow him to climb up with more ease.

Wooden Warnings

Not all wood is created equal. When selecting pieces to use as shelves and branches in your iguana's cage, you must be sure to pick those that are safe to use. Any pieces of wood that are leaking saps or resins are out. These could be toxic, irritating, or just sticky. In any event, you don't want to use them. In particular, pines, cedars, and other similar trees should be avoided. Try to use only hardwoods, though these are more expensive.

If you are purchasing your wood from building-supply stores, be sure that the wood has not been treated with arsenic-bearing preservatives. While it is not proven these preservatives are dangerous, I advise against putting anything laden with arsenic in an iguana cage. Your ig will certainly taste it on occasion and there may even be fumes. I can't imagine this is healthy for him— or even for you when you are cleaning the cage.

If you collect your branches from outside, there is a strong possibility other critters could come along with the wood. Mites, ants, centipedes, spiders, and other undesirables may be living in the wood and come out later to explore the new surroundings. Some of them may be dangerous to your iguana or other members of your household. Additionally, a piece of wood that has been sitting outside for any length of time might be hosting any number of molds, fungi, bacteria, protozoans, and other potential pathogens. You will need to get rid of these before you move the branches into your ig's home.

There are a couple of ways to go about getting rid of any unwanted hitchhikers on your branches. You can soak the wood in bleach and water for a half-hour or so. This should kill almost anything living on or in the wood. Afterward, you must rinse the wood thoroughly until there is no smell of bleach left. Then, allow the wood to dry in the sun before use. Another method is to wrap the wood in aluminum foil and bake in the oven for an hour or so. After it cools down, remove the foil and use it in the cage.

Safety

All limbs, perches, and roosts must be well secured. I cannot emphasize this enough. The last thing you want is to have a limb or shelf detach from the side of the cage and come crashing down on top of your iguana. Iguanas have been killed by improperly secured branches; don't let that happen to your scaly friend.

How you attach the perches and such depends on the type of cage you have. It is most difficult in a glass aquarium: there is really nothing to attach anything to. In this case, you can use silicon sealant or a non-toxic epoxy to affix the branches to the sides of the cage. This will increase the difficulty of cleaning the cage, but there may be little choice. If you can find pieces of wood that wedge into the space, that may work. Be very careful about this; an active iguana may dislodge the perches, particularly as he grows larger and stronger.

Branches and vines should be secured tightly to the enclosure's sides.

Another option for securely attaching perches when housing your iguana in an aquarium is to suspend

Iguanas feel most safe when they are at least several feet off of the ground on branches or shelves.

the perches from the screen-cage top. To do this, you must buy one of the sturdier screen lids. Once you have that, you can use a natural fiber twine to suspend a couple of branches or platforms at various heights. Make sure your iguana can reach all of them or all you have done is create some strange decorations for the cage. Be careful that the lights are not close enough to the twine to start a fire.

In wooden cages, you can drill holes in the perches and screw them directly to the walls of the cage. I advise screws over nails, as they can be removed and reattached easily for maintenance, redecorating, or moving. The same can be done with a Plexiglas cage, but care must be taken to avoid damaging the Plexiglas.

If your cage is made primarily of wire, you can wire the branches to the sides of the cage. Be careful there are no bits of wires that could puncture or strangle your ig. In my wood and wire cage, I used boards and some thick tree limbs as columns and placed the main basking shelf on top of them. They are nailed (I wish I had thought to use screws) to the sides of the cage and then wired in place for additional stability. A long branch runs from the floor of the cage diagonally up to the shelf. It is nailed (again, I should've used screws) to the cage floor, wired to the side of the cage, and nailed to the column supporting the basking roost.

If you have some other cage type not covered here, use these ideas as guidelines. With some ingenuity, you should be able to figure out how to make the limbs and shelves in the enclosure both safe and functional for your iguana.

Hide Boxes

Most first-time iguana owners do not use hide boxes, caves, or any other method of giving their iguana a little privacy. I think this is because most pet stores do not inform first-time owners of an iguana's need to feel safe and secure. This is a shame, because having a hide box can reduce the occurrence of aggressive and panicky behaviors in new iguanas.

For these reasons, I recommend giving your iguana some area to be out of view. Iguanas–even adults–are hunted by many creatures in the wild. They like to be able to get out of sight periodically. A healthy and acclimated iguana will probably not use his hide box much, but one should be included for the times he feels the need to get out of the public eye for a while.

For newly purchased baby iguanas or any iguana that is new to your home, you should consider the use of a hide box essential. Moving into a new home is stressful for humans; imagine how stressful it must be for an iguana that has no idea what is going on or where he is. Having a place to go to be out of sight will help keep them from getting overly stressed, aggressive, and panicky.

A hide box can be any type of shelter that screens your iguana from view. It should be large enough to comfortably fit his body (it's okay if the tail has to curl up to fit in the box), but it should not be so big that he cannot touch the walls of the box. Iguanas, like most reptiles, like a fairly tight-fitting hiding area. It probably makes them feel more secure that they can touch the entire inside of the box (this makes some sense, because that way they can be sure no nasty predator is in the box with them). The hide box must have a way your iguana can get in and out easily. It should also be easy for you to get your iguana out of his hide box when you need to. There should be no sharp edges or other surfaces that could cause your iguana injury. Lastly, the hide box must be easy to clean and sterilize.

Green iguanas should be offered shade in which to relieve themselves from the intensity of heat lamps.

Over the years, herpers have used numerous different materials for hide boxes. Hollow logs and pieces of bark are widely used. They look nice but often are hard to clean. You can find attractive stone and faux-stone (usually some type of plastic or resin) caves at many pet stores and herp shows. There are also some very realistic, fake wooden ones. These give you a natural look but normally are easier to clean than their natural counterparts, though the natural materials tend to be less expensive than the artificial ones.

If you are not worried about having a natural look to your enclosure, you have lots of options. Cardboard boxes work and have the advantage of being disposable (you can even use cereal boxes for small igs). Lengths of PVC pipe of a diameter appropriate for your iguana are inexpensive, durable, and easy to clean. You can even cut them to fit wherever in the cage you want to put them. PVC pipe can be painted to blend in with the cage, if you desire. Be sure to use a nontoxic paint. Because PVC pipes come in large diameters, they can be used with adult iguanas.

Plastic food storage containers with entry holes cut in them have been a favorite with herpers for years, although they are not useful for large iguanas. I recommend painting them a dark color to screen out most of the light. After all, the point of the hide box is to give your iguana a place that is out of view. For larger iguanas, you could use covered kitty litter pans, dishpans, or plastic storage tubs. I created a hide box/nesting box for my iguanas out of a plastic kitchen garbage pail.

Plants

Plants–real or artificial–spruce up any herp enclosure. They give the human viewer a sense that there is a little slice of nature in the terrarium. Unfortunately, keeping plants in an iguana enclosure usually does not work.

Live Plants

Plants provide a natural perch for green iguanas and often bring out their best colors.

Many keepers start out by thinking that, because iguanas are herbivores, keeping real, edible plants in the cage would be a good idea. They fail to predict how quickly an iguana will destroy or consume a plant. The beautiful hibiscus tree you bought just for your iguana cage will look like the sad victim of a locust swarm in only a couple of days. If your iguana chooses not to eat the plant, he will certainly climb on it. This will result in sliced up leaves, broken branches, and flattened stems.

Real plants may even present a danger to your ig. Many houseplants are irritating, toxic, or injurious to iguanas. If you pick the wrong plant, your iguana may end up hurt, sick, or even dead. Even plants that are edible are often treated with pesticides, fungicides, fertilizers, and other chemicals, some of which could harm your ig. There is also the possibility your ig will eat some of the potting soil, which could cause gut impactions or exposure to pesticides and fertilizers.

Artificial Plants

Artificial plants may be a better choice, but using them comes with other problems. There are some very nice, naturalistic fake plants on the market these days. Some of the best are made of silk or high-quality plastic. They will hold up better than a real plant, but they are still no match for the trampling an iguana will dish out to them. You will have to replace them, probably at least once a year.

Avoid the cheaper fake plants that have the bending wire running through the stems. After some wear, the wire often pokes through the stem. Your iguana can get punctured on the stem. It's possible that he could even lose an eye, if the wire hit him correctly.

Solo Iguana

You may notice I refer to housing one iguana, not groups of them. This is because I highly recommend having only one iguana. Iguanas often do not get along, and even those that have been fine and friendly together can suddenly start fighting. In captivity there is not enough space for the loser to get away from the winner. Eventually, the loser usually dies, if not from injuries from the dominant iguana then from the stress of being forced to cohabitate with the bully.

Iguanas kept singly and given plenty of attention from their owners become the best pets. Having a second or third iguana lessens the importance of the ig's relationship to his owner. For these reasons, I do not recommend keeping more than one iguana.

Some keepers worry that their iguanas will try to eat the fake plants. Most iguanas do try to sample the plants, but after a small nibble they realize these plants are tough to chew and do not taste good. This will not stop some iguanas, however. If you introduce artificial plants to the enclosure, keep a good eye on what happens at first. If your iguana starts to eat them, get them out of the cage immediately.

In the end, it is probably best to avoid plants altogether. They generally prove to be more trouble than they are worth.

Part 2

Warning:
Aquarium + Sunlight = Oven

If you house your iguana in an aquarium, you must be careful about sunlight. The glass easily lets in light and heat but traps the heat inside. This can quickly cause a buildup of heat, resulting in a dramatic rise in temperature, which, in turn, results in a dead iguana. Think of the warnings you've heard about dogs in cars on hot days; the same logic applies. When positioning the aquarium, be sure to keep it out of direct sunlight. When you want to give your iguana some sun, take him out of the aquarium.

Other Choices

If you still want that natural look to your enclosure, there are a few alternatives. You could buy some of the aquarium backgrounds often sold in pet stores and attach them to the back of your enclosure. This will probably be expensive, but it will look nice. If you know someone with some artistic ability, they could paint areas of the enclosure or the walls behind with some nice jungle scenes. This is not only visually appealing, but it also adds a unique touch to your iguana's enclosure. In a large enclosure, you could have live or artificial plants that are out of your iguana's reach but still visible to the viewer. You could do this by placing them behind the cage, in their own screened-off area, up on iguana-proof pedestals, or hanging on the outside of the enclosure.

Other ways of making your enclosure look more like the rainforest are limited only by your imagination and the needs of your iguana.

Litter Pan

If you are new to iguanas, it may seem strange that you would want a litter pan in your ig's enclosure. However, having a litter pan will decrease the frequency with which you have to clean out the whole cage.

You can use any of the recommended substrates as the litter. I favor recycled paper bedding, but shredded newspaper, paper towels, mulch, and other materials will work fine. Avoid anything the iguana might ingest and anything that will rot quickly (such as alfalfa pellets). See the substrates section for some ideas. Under no circumstances use kitty litter or corncob as the litter. Both of these substances create a high risk of gut impactions.

For a litter box, you want to use something that your iguana can fit most of his body into and that he can get in and out of easily. The pan should not be prone to tipping over–

although a really upset iguana will be able to flip over most pans if he decides to do so. Wide and low kitty-litter pans are ideal, but large dishpans can be used. Creative people may find other options.

At this point you are likely saying to yourself, "But how do I get my iguana to use his litter pan?" The answer lies in your iguana's own behavior. Most iguanas will pick a spot in their cage and do their business in that spot preferentially. If you put a litter pan in that spot, your ig will most likely continue to use the spot and go in the pan. Using some form of scoop, pick out the waste on a daily basis and replace the entire pan as needed (usually once a week, but it varies). When you do your weekly pan cleaning, you should use a bleach solution to disinfect it at the same time. Soak the pan in a solution of bleach and water for at least 15 minutes, and then rinse it thoroughly. Dry it, refill it, and return it to the chosen spot.

If your iguana decides not to use the pan, there could be any number of reasons. He may not like the litter or the shape, color, size, or smell of the pan. Try a different pan and a different litter. You should eventually come up with a combination your iguana finds acceptable.

Despite providing a nice, sanitary litter pan for your iguana, he may still prefer to use his water bowl. There may be little you can do about this. One idea is to suspend the water bowl above the cage floor, but this creates other logistical problems (daily filling becomes a chore). If you choose to try it, make sure the bowl cannot be tipped easily and that your ig can still drink from it. One way to do this involves having two bowls. One of the bowls is epoxied or otherwise attached to one of the roosting platforms. The second nests inside the other bowl. This prevents most spills yet still allows for you to easily remove and clean the bowl.

If your iguana persists in defecating in his water bowl, you'll have to resign yourself to cleaning it every day. You should dump the fouled water in your toilet–not a sink that you or family members use. Bleach out the bowl and rinse it thoroughly before refilling it.

Where to Put the Cage

You will do best with your iguana if you don't just stick the cage any place you have the room for it. Even the best-designed cage providing a perfect habitat for your ig will be less than perfect if it is positioned in a bad spot.

Cage placement is very important; be sure to avoid drafty locations and areas frequented by many people.

So what makes a bad spot for an iguana enclosure? A number of things, actually. First, you want to put the enclosure in an area that is free of drafts. A cool draft blowing into the cage will make it difficult to keep the temperature in the preferred range and could lead to your iguana developing illnesses.

While some sunlight is good, the enclosure should be in an area that is not fully illuminated by sunlight at any point during the day. What I mean here is that the iguana should be able to get out of the sun when he gets too hot. Also, be aware that direct sunlight will increase the cage temperature dramatically; plan on this when you are designing the cage. You can use thermostats to turn off the heat lamps, etc., when sunlight makes the temperature too high. Never put an aquarium in the direct sunlight; you will quickly fry your poor iguana.

Another bad spot for an iguana cage is a high-traffic area in the house. Your iguana, especially when he's new to your home, will be stressed out by all the comings and goings, noise, motion, etc.

Conversely, do not put the iguana cage in an area of the house where no one ever goes. Iguanas do like to see some activity and will become bored if there is nothing to watch. Additionally, the more the cage is out of the way, the less often you will be likely to take your iguana out of the cage and interact with him. This is the prescription for a socially maladjusted iguana. So, no iguana enclosures in garages, basements, out-of-the-way closets, unused hallways, and other such places.

Cleaning and Sanitation

The downside to owning any animal—be it mammal, reptile, bird, or fish—is that you have to clean up after it. Most animals do not know how to clean up their own wastes, so it is up to the owner to do it for them. Iguanas are no different.

If your iguana uses his litter pan, your daily cleaning chore is pretty easy. You scoop out the soiled area or dump out the whole pan, depending on the type of litter you use. Then you replace it in the cage. Once a week, you should remove the pan and soak it in bleach and water for 15 minutes or more. Then rinse it well, dry it, add the litter, and put it back in the cage.

Daily Duties

Each day, you should check the cage for cleanliness. You are looking for bits of food, pieces of shed skin, stray wastes not in the pan, or anything else that compromises the hygiene of the enclosure. Remove the offending items and those sections of substrate, if necessary. Most of the time, your iguana will just go in the pan and you will only have a couple of pieces of food to pick up.

Also, look at your iguana daily and see if he has bits of food stuck to his mouth or smeared feces anywhere on his body. You will see both of these more often if you are feeding your iguana fruit in any quantity, but it occasionally happens no matter what the diet. Food can be removed from the mouth and face by using a damp cloth or cotton swab. You can remove smeared feces the same way. Afterward, you must be sure to wash the cloth in hot, bleachy water separate from any family laundry. I keep all my reptile-related laundry together in a plastic bag and do a whole load of it. This cuts down a little on laundry because I'm not running the washer just to do two soiled cloths.

When my iguanas get themselves messy, I soak them in the tub prior to using a cloth. The soak softens up the material, making removal easier. I then bleach the tub and cloths together. I have cloths that are designated solely for use with the iguanas, and I recommend you do the same to help prevent any possible bouts with salmonella.

Iguanas kept in cages that are too small for them are much more likely to foul their cage and result

Daily Care

Turn on the lights or make sure your timer turned the lights on at the proper time.

Check that all lights, heaters, humidifiers, and thermostats are working correctly. Check the temperatures at various spots in the cage.

Observe your iguana for signs of illness or other problems (food stuck to mouth, etc.).

Spot-clean cage and/or litter pan as needed.

Clean out water bowl and refill.

Dump any uneaten food out of the bowl. Prepare fresh food and refill the bowl.

Take your iguana out of enclosure for socialization and exercise.

in more frequent cleaning by the keeper—along with greater risk the iguana and the keeper will become ill. This is because in a small cage there is little space available for your iguana to avoid stepping in and tracking around his wastes. Here is yet another reason to provide your iguana with ample space.

Weekly Scrub-Down

You should do a more thorough cleaning of the enclosure weekly or as needed (like when your iguana kicks the litter pan all over the cage and walks through it—always on the day after you just did the major weekly cleaning). This involves removing all the removable parts of the cage (branches, bowls, perches, litter pans, etc.) and washing them in hot, soapy water. Leaving them to soak helps. You want to remove all organic wastes. Once they are completely cleaned, you have to rinse off all of the soap.

At this time, you should also wash the entire cage the same way (hot, soapy water and thorough rinsing). Again, you don't want to leave behind any wastes. If you find some items that are really stuck on, you can use a dull knife or spatula to scrap off the material. Make sure this item is only used for iguana cleanup and never for any human-related use. The sponges, cloths, and towels you use for cage cleaning should also be used only for that purpose. You can do this through color-coding (I use only green sponges for herp cleaning), by storing everything in one bucket, or any other method that keeps you from mixing up iguana-cleaning items with human-cleaning items.

Antibacterial soaps?

It seems every soap on the market these days is labeled antibacterial. However, these are not the same as disinfectants. Disinfectants are much more powerful destroyers of germs. It is alright to use antibacterial soaps for the washing process, but their use does not replace the use of disinfectants.

After the washing and rinsing, all items and the cage interior should be disinfected. Cleaning removes the actual physical dirt: wastes, shed skins, food, and other materials. Disinfection kills off the microbes (bacteria, viruses, molds, etc.) that could cause illness. There are many disinfectants on the market. The two I like best are household bleach and Nolvasan, a veterinary disinfectant (your vet should be able to get it or a generic form for you, or you can try the Internet). Nolvasan is less harsh and less potentially harmful than bleach, but it is much more expensive.

To make the bleach solution for disinfecting the cage, add one-part bleach to eight or nine parts water. If you use

Nolvasan or some other commercial disinfectant, follow the instructions on the bottle. Spray all areas of the cage and furnishings with the disinfectant and allow them to sit for at least 15 minutes. Small cage items, such as the food and water bowls, can be immersed in the disinfectant and left to soak for this time.

Once the disinfectant has been left to stand on the cage surfaces for 15 minutes, you should rinse them off and place them back in the cage. If you use bleach, you *must* rinse the cage and cage furnishings thoroughly and allow them to dry before allowing your iguana near them. Thoroughly rinsing means that there is no smell of bleach left in the cage or on the cage furnishings. You do not need to be this careful with Nolvasan; a light rinsing will be adequate.

> ## Weekly Care
>
> Clean and disinfect food and water bowls.
>
> Clean and disinfect all enclosure furnishings.
>
> Clean and disinfect the enclosure itself.
>
> Soak your iguana for at least 30 minutes.
>
> Check your iguana's claws and trim if needed.
>
> Check your iguana's spines. If any have shed skin stuck to them, gently remove it.
>
> Look at your iguana's toes. If there are strands of carpet wrapped around them, gently remove them.

You may be wondering what to do with your iguana while you strip down and clean out his home. There are a couple of options. This is a great time to let him roam a bit in an iguana-proof space. Just be sure to keep him away from the cleaning supplies and hot water. Another option would be to do his weekly soaking time while you do the weekly cleaning. Remember to check on him periodically during his soak; don't get so caught-up in the cleaning that you forget your iguana is in the tub. If you have a cage for putting him out in the sunlight on a nice day, you can move your iguana out there when you clean. If all else fails, you can put your ig in a large cat or dog carrier, but this is certainly the least appealing option, especially from your iguana's point of view.

Irregular Cleaning

Along with the weekly and daily cleaning, there are assorted cleaning chores that you want to perform as needed. You should wipe the dust and dirt off the heat lamps and power cords periodically, always remembering to unplug them and let them cool first. Every month or so, you should move the enclosure and clean underneath it (it's amazing–and sometimes gross–what you find beneath an iguana cage). If you use a humidifier in your cage, you should clean and disinfect that according to the manufacturer's instructions (if there are no guidelines, I would recommend doing this once a week or once every other week). The outside surfaces of the enclosure can be cleaned weekly or as needed.

4

The World Outside

Taking Your Iguana Outdoors

Many keepers like the idea of taking their iguanas outside with them. They know the benefits of exposing their green friend to natural sunlight, and they think it will be fun to take him along. Other keepers want to house their iguanas outside–all the time or at least on nice days.

It is fine to give your iguana a taste of the great outdoors, but there are ways to do it safely and there are ways that make it likely your iguana will escape or be harmed. This chapter will discuss making the outdoors as safe as possible for your iguana.

Iguanas can be exposed to the outdoors as long as the temperature is warm.

Outdoor Warning

Do not house your iguana outside if the temperatures are not warm enough. The nighttime temperatures should be at least 65∞F. If not, you'll have to bring you ig inside at night. Daytime temperatures should be at least 80∞F. At times of the year when it is not this warm, your iguana must be brought indoors and placed in a properly outfitted cage.

Outdoor Housing

If you live in a warm climate, you might be considering housing your iguana outdoors. If you live in the temperate zone, you may be thinking that you could house your iguana outside for the summer. This section will talk about how to keep your iguana outside and the potential problems you and he will face.

The Good: Benefits of Outdoor Housing

There are a number of reasons why housing your iguana outdoors is a good idea. One of these is the size of enclosure you can offer him. When you are not limited by the considerations of your living space, you can probably devote more space to the iguana enclosure than you could indoors. Your iguana will love having all that space; as we discussed, iguanas do not like to be cramped.

The biggest benefit to housing your iguana outdoors is the exposure to natural sunlight. There is no artificial light that compares to sunlight, and outdoors your iguana will get as much of it as he wants and needs. It has been noted that iguanas housed outdoors are often more intensely colored than their indoor brethren. This probably is due largely to their exposure to sunlight. Iguanas kept outdoors almost never develop metabolic bone disease; those few that do are being fed an improper diet.

An iguana housed outdoors probably has more to see than one kept indoors. He can watch the movement of leaves in the wind, the flying birds, insects, even your neighbor mowing the lawn. Iguanas like to watch things, and being outdoors gives them more visual stimuli than is usually possible indoors.

If you have a green thumb, you can grow nutritious plants in and near the enclosure. This allows your iguana to do some of his own foraging and enriches his life. Even if you can't grow anything, he's sure to nibble on any grasses or weeds in his domain.

The Bad: Drawbacks to Outdoor Housing

While there are significant benefits to housing your iguana outdoors, there are also drawbacks and associated hazards. You have to weigh both the benefits and the hazards and decide if it is worth it to you. I think most iguana owners would house their iguanas outdoors for at least part of the year if they could, but only you can decide whether such a situation is right for you and your iguana.

Probably the biggest problem with outdoor housing of your green guy is protecting him from other animals–not to mention malicious humans. Most neighborhoods have at least one of these threats to your iguana roaming about: raccoons, opossums, hawks, dogs, cats, rats, and coyotes. Any of these animals could make a snack of your iguana or one of his parts. (I say that because I heard of a keeper whose iguana had his foot gnawed off by a rat when he was housed outdoors.) There are ways of protecting your iguana, but none of them are completely foolproof.

Aside from predators, there are also other living hazards, namely pathogens and parasites. Indoor iguanas have few opportunities for picking up these nasties. Outdoor iguanas are much more likely to be exposed to disease-causing organisms. If you house your iguana outside, you have to monitor his health carefully. Visits to the vet once to twice yearly are a must (of course, your iguana should get a yearly checkup whether he is outdoors or not).

Another problem is inclement weather. You have to be prepared to move your iguana indoors should the weather get bad or at least provide him with areas that are shielded from the elements.

Iguanas housed outdoors often are less adapted to human contact than those kept indoors.

Outwitting Ants

If you end up with an ant invasion in your outdoor cage or sunning cage, you'll need to correct the problem fast. Ants can injure or even kill an iguana quicker than you would believe. They seem to be more of a problem for keepers of slower-moving lizards (such as chameleons), but they still can present a real hazard to igs.

The easiest way to beat ants is to put the legs of your cage in cans or other containers that are partially filled with some type of oil (olive, cooking, corn, etc.). The ants cannot cross the surface and will drown in the oil. I've heard that soapy water works as well, so you could also try that.

When you are putting the legs in the containers, make sure they are in the middle of the oil container and not touching the sides. If they are touching the sides, the ants can still climb right up them and avoid the oil.

Part 2

Chicken wire or hardware cloth is suitable outdoor cage material as long as you provide shade.

This could be because of the sunlight or it could be because when the iguana is outdoors the keeper spends less time with him. In any case, it is true that many iguanas kept outside are more frightful of or aggressive toward humans than those housed inside.

Building the Outdoor Cage

Once you decide to go ahead and house your iguana outdoors, you have to build a cage. There are a number of ways to do this and several materials you could use. Here, we'll talk about what you need for such a cage and ways around the hazards discussed in the previous section.

In some ways, designing the outdoor cage is simpler than designing the indoor cage. The outdoor enclosure has no need for heating and lighting. The sun provides all of that, so you are freed from positioning things in ways that allow your iguana proximity to the UV. Your ig will get plenty of UV from the sunlight streaming into the enclosure.

Floor or No Floor

There are two basic approaches to outdoor cages. You can use the ground as the floor of the cage or you could build a floor. The ground-floor enclosure is a little easier to build and allows your iguana to graze on grasses and such—at least until he devours all of the plants in his cage. It is easier to keep the ground-floor cage clean than it is with a floor you build. However, your iguana might someday dig himself out of the cage or an unwanted visitor might dig its way in. Also, being on the ground exposes your iguana to ants, other bugs, and possibly pathogens and parasites.

To make the ground-floor cage safer, you should turn the soil over before building the cage. Another option would be to buy sterile, organic topsoil and cover the floor space with it to a depth of several inches. Do not use any pesticides or such to try to make the area free of bugs.

If you build a floor into your cage, you avoid many of the hazards of the ground-floor cage.

Note that, unless you elevate the enclosure on legs, you still may have problems with ants and other vermin. It is recommended that you elevate the cage at least 2 feet. This may be impractical with a very large cage.

Most outdoor cages are built of wood and wire. You should use a sturdy wire, such as hardware cloth, as this will help keep out predators. The wire must not have any sharp pieces that could injure your iguana, and the mesh size must be fairly small (no bigger than quarter-inch). Rubberized wire is probably the best way to go. You really want to get the sturdiest wire you can afford because it has to serve the double duty of keeping your iguana in and keeping undesirable animals out.

Preventing Iguana Excavations

If you build your outdoor cage using the ground for the floor, your iguana could dig out. Most iguanas won't, but it has happened. This is especially true if the iguana is a female who happens to be gravid (pregnant) or if the weather gets unexpectedly cold. However, simple boredom could cause your iguana to dig a tunnel to freedom.

The easiest way to prevent this in a dirt-floored cage is to dig down below the surface and sink the wire mesh 6 to 12 inches. Once the iguana realizes he can get no further, he'll abandon the project. Just to be safe, fill in any hole as soon as you notice it.

Part 2

The Door

When constructing the cage, make the door just as sturdy as the rest of the cage if not more so. The door is the weakest point, so it pays to put some time into making sure it is secure. I recommend some form of lock for it, even if it is just a hook-and-eye latch. You have to prevent your iguana from pushing out and other creatures from prying in. A latch at the top of the door and one at the bottom are recommended.

While on this subject, I want to recommend that you have a fenced-in yard. This helps prevent some bad things from happening. It can help keep your iguana contained if he should escape the outdoor cage. A fence also helps keep predators out of your yard and away from your pet. Finally, a fence may deter any humans with iguana-related mischief on their minds. It's sad that you need to consider that, but you do.

Comforts

Your iguana needs to have drinking water at all times when outdoors. This applies indoors, also, but is especially critical in the outdoor cage. He should also be fed as normal. Because he'll be getting more sunlight and probably be more active, you may find you have to feed your ig more food when he is kept outdoors.

Remember that your iguana likes to stay above the ground. You have to provide the same types of perches, shelves, and limbs that you would include in the indoor cage. If you include enough climbing areas, it may keep your ig from climbing on the wire of the cage. Climbing the cage wire will wear on the cage over time. Also, iguanas have been known to break their toes in wire mesh. Giving him ample opportunities to climb without resorting to the wire will prevent both of these problems.

Protection from the Elements

The roof of the cage should be about three-quarters wire–to let sunlight in–and one-quarter wood, plastic, tin, or some other opaque substance–to block out some sunlight. Position the opaque panel so that there is always a mix of sun and shade in the enclosure. Remember that iguanas can overheat. You have to provide your iguana with opportunities to get out of the sun if he gets too hot. To further provide some shade, you could use boards (about 3 feet tall) around the bottom of one or two walls of the enclosure. These will create some more shady areas.

To further give your iguana an opportunity to escape the heat, provide a water basin he can soak in. This can be a child's wading pool, a dishpan, or anything else that your iguana can fit into. On very hot days, some keepers position their garden sprinkler so that it sprays the enclosure. This is fine, but you must be careful it does not soak the whole cage. If your iguana wants to be dry and in the sun, he should have that opportunity. Be forewarned that some iguanas are scared of sprinklers.

What if the weather gets too cold? The best response to the cold weather is to bring your iguana indoors. However, if you can't do that for some reason, you can get him through a brief cold snap in his outdoor cage with some careful planning. Note that he *should never be outdoors if the temperature is going to be below 50°F.* If the temperature is going to stay below 70°F for more than a day or two at most, you have to bring your ig inside.

To get your iguana through a short cold snap, you need to have some equipment ready to use: plastic sheeting, outdoor-safe extension cords, spare heat lamps, and high-wattage bulbs. These things can save your iguana from freezing in a pinch. First, wrap as much of the cage as possible in the plastic sheeting. You can secure it with duct tape, clothespins, or whatever you have handy that will do the job. Set up one or more basking lights over a convenient roost. Make sure that they do not rest against the plastic sheeting, as they might get hot enough to melt it. Plug them into the extension cords and leave them on until the cold weather lets up. You may even move your iguana to the basking spot to be sure he gets to the warmth before becoming too cold to move. Between the sheeting and the lamps, your ig should be warm enough to make it through a mild cold snap.

Another way of providing for a cold snap and keeping your iguana outdoors is to use a large dog carrier, the ones used to take your dog on an airplane, made mostly out of plastic and having a screen metal door. Place this in the outdoor enclosure with some form of substrate on the bottom. Put your iguana inside of it and position a heat lamp so that it shines in the metal door. Again, this is far from an ideal situation, but it will keep your ig alive and mostly fine through a cold spell.

The Sunning Cage

This is a variation on outdoor housing. It differs in being a smaller cage you use to just get your iguana outside on bright, sunny days.

This cage can be built in the same fashion as the regular outdoor cage. However, because your iguana will only be in it for a few hours at a time, it does not need to be big. It should still be large enough for him to move around, but you don't need to think about giving him all the space that is normally recommended.

The sunning cage does, however, need to provide a proper environment for your ig. You must have climbing branches, shady areas, food, and water available.

At some herp shows, you can find vendors who make outdoor chameleon cages. These may be suited for your iguana, too. Check the size and sturdiness. If you find a vendor who makes nice

Sunning cages are almost always made of wire mesh or a similar material.

Part 2

chameleon cages, you might be able to have him or her make an iguana sunning cage for you. It may cost a bit, but if you aren't handy or you like the person's design, it will be well worth it.

One feature that it is a good idea to include on the sunning cage is wheels. This way you can wheel it out to a porch or patio whenever you want to give your ig some sunshine. You can also move it as the day progresses to keep your ig happily in the sun. Just remember what we've said about the importance of shade.

Outside, Out of Cage

There may be times that you want to take your iguana outside but not have him in a cage. I recommend resisting this impulse. This is how many iguanas get lost. You may think that you will keep your eye on him the whole time you are outside, but when the phone rings, the neighbor leans over the fence to chat, or some other distraction pops up, your iguana could make a break for it. If you think your iguana would never do that, think again—and again. Iguanas are not

Because iguanas are very fast, it is important to provide adequate supervision when they are outside.

Toxic Weeds

When your iguana is housed outdoors, you have to be sure no toxic plants are within snacking range. Grasses are harmless, but some pretty common weeds are toxic. Consult a book on gardening or one of the online poisonous plants lists. Some common ones to look for are Queen Anne's lace, azaleas, woody nightshade, lily-of-the-valley, toadstools, some ivies, and yews. This list is far from complete, and you are encouraged to do some research to determine what is growing in or near your iguana's enclosure. Obviously, you also want to get rid of any plants that have spines or thorns.

domesticated, no matter how well you've socialized yours. They will seek to exhibit wild behaviors when they can, including exploring new turf for food or mates and climbing to the tops of tall trees.

One option you can try is to use one of the iguana harnesses available in many pet stores. Most iguanas do not like them and may never adapt to wearing one. I tried Kermit on a leash several times. She was fine until the leash got taut. Then she would hiss and flail around as though she was possessed. After a couple of tries, I gave up. Other iguana keepers report serious or more violent reactions. Others say that their iguana won't move when the harness is on and the lizard goes into an almost catatonic state.

However, some iguanas do not seem to mind. Note that most of the harnesses available are not safe for babies. They are too big, and a baby will slip right out of one. You probably need to wait until your iguana is at least a year old before you can use a leash and harness.

Be sure to buy a harness that does not go across the throat of your ig. This can not only cause damage to the trachea if your iguana gets too frisky, but it may also damage the hyoid bone that controls dewlap and tongue motility.

It is also wise to test the harness and leash indoors several times before going outside with your iguana attached to it. It is far better to discover that your ig can escape from his leash when you are inside than when you are outdoors.

The Traveling Iguana

There are times when you may have to take your iguana on a trip. This could be a simple trip to the vet or a cross-country move. In either case or with something in-between those two extremes, you need to keep your iguana safe and happy on the trip.

By Car

For trips by car, you will need to buy a pet carrier of a size big enough for your iguana to fit inside. It is alright if his tail has to curve around a little, but it should fit him as comfortably as possible. The Nylabone® Fold-Away Pet Carrier is a perfect pet carrier to use for this purpose. When I moved from upstate New York to New Jersey, I bought the largest size dog crate available to put Petey and Kermit inside for the trip. They could just fit inside of it. This should give you some idea of what you need.

The carrier should be secured in the car with a seatbelt or bungee cords. You really don't want it sliding around or being thrown from the seat when you stop suddenly. If you are moving, you can pack your boxes and bags around the carrier to prevent it from moving. If you do this, be sure you don't cover up the ventilation openings.

You should line the bottom of the carrier with paper towels or some other easy to clean and absorbent substrate. It is certainly possible your iguana will choose to defecate during the trip. This goes for short trips as well as long ones. Sometimes I think iguanas just like to eliminate anywhere that is not their own cage.

While on the trip, keep the car at a comfortable temperature for your iguanas. This probably means you will be warm, but you are less likely to suffer any ill effects from being too warm than the iguana is if he is too cool. However, if you have to take your ig for a ride on a hot, sunny day, be aware that sunlight coming through a window and into the carrier can overheat him. Check on your iguana periodically to see if you need to put on the air conditioner or move the carrier to a less sunny spot.

On long car trips, you will need to schedule stops for feeding and watering your ig. Highway rest areas are usually good for this. Just be careful not to let your ig get away.

You may think of letting your iguana free in the car as you drive. This is dangerous for you, your ig, and other drivers. If your iguana jumps on you, gets under your feet, or distracts you in some way, you could have an accident. If you need to stop suddenly, your poor ig could get flung across the car, possibly breaking a bone or suffering some other injury.

I tried to travel once with Kermit free in the car. I put her up in the back window above the back seat. She stayed there seemingly content for most of the trip. However, she suddenly leapt from the back window to the back of the driver seat, burying several claws in the back of my head. If someone had been close behind me, I would've been rear-ended, as I slammed on the brakes. I've also heard of iguanas getting lost inside of the dashboard or in the seats. Never let your iguana loose in the car.

By Public Transportation

There may come a time in your life when you need to take your iguana on a trip by bus, plane, or train. There are special considerations you must make when traveling with your iguana by one of these media.

The first thing to consider is whether or not your iguana will be welcome by the company in charge of the vehicle. Most buses probably will not allow your iguana on board, while most planes and trains will have strict rules about how your iguana can be transported. For the most part, these rules will restrict you from taking your iguana into the passenger areas. Your iguana will probably ride with the freight in his carrier. This is not ideal, but it is the standard.

Iguana-Phobia

It may come as a surprise to an iguana-lover, but most people in the public at large do not like iguanas. In fact, many people are actually scared of them. For this reason, it is irresponsible to take your iguana into a public setting where people do not expect to see iguanas. This means it is really best for everyone if you do not take your iguana to the park or public beach. Keeping your iguana out of the public eye prevents confrontations and hard feelings. If you take your iguana out in public and someone gets frightened enough, they may go to their town council or local legislative body and try to have the keeping of reptiles or exotic pets banned. This has indeed happened in some areas. Even if such dire consequences do not occur, taking your iguana into an area where he is not welcome further sours relations between the herp and non-herp communities. Please, be responsible and realize that you represent all herp keepers to the public at times.

I have heard many horror stories about iguanas and other animals on airplanes. I've heard of several owners whose pets were lost (as in the airline had no idea where the pets were sent) and others whose pets actually died from being left on hot tarmac or out in the cold. I would never take my animals on a commercial airliner. Other people do take their pets on airplanes without incident, but it scares me too much.

I would like to discourage you from sneaking your iguana onto a plane or train. If you are discovered, you may be fined or your poor ig may even be confiscated. You certainly will cause a stir from the passengers and the staff–and probably not a good stir. This is not only bad for you and your ig, it makes all iguana and reptile keepers look like irresponsible show-offs. Please follow the rules on public transportation.

Inappropriate Places

There are a number of places where it is never okay to take your iguana, no matter how cute and well behaved he is. These include any place pets are not welcome, like hospitals, office buildings, and such. I once brought an iguana into a bookstore and was immediately asked to leave (I was young and foolish). So, any place with a "No Pets" policy includes your ig. Any type of business serving food will not welcome your iguana. In fact, bringing him there creates a health hazard for others. These places include grocery stores, restaurants, fast-food places, and health food stores, among others.

Although it is fine to take you iguana to friends' houses—as long as the friend doesn't mind—you should never take your iguana to the home of a friend who has a baby, who has a compromised immune system, or who lives with someone who does. You do not want your iguana to be the cause of an illness or worse tragedy.

Part Three

Feeding the Beast

MPIFER © 2004

"Of course, I only eat light salads these days.
Have to watch my figure, and all."

Diet, Nutrition, and Feeding

One of the questions I am most frequently asked about iguanas is "What do they eat?" Some folks offer a guess, usually suggesting mice or crickets. It is true that many other reptiles eat something similar to mice or crickets, and it must be one of these species of which the questioner is thinking. However, iguanas do not eat (or should not, actually) mice or crickets–they eat plants. One of the nice things about keeping iguanas is that you never have to feed him live animals. Actually, you never have to go to a pet store to buy your iguana food; you can buy all the items right in a grocery store or neighborhood farm market.

An adult male green iguana needs a well-balanced diet that is high in plant proteins.

Calcium, Calcium, Calcium

Not all plants are created equal. You will want to feed your iguana the most nutritious types and avoid some that lack nutrients or contain substances that may be detrimental to his health. Of particular concern is calcium, or actually, the ratio of calcium to phosphorus. An iguana should consume at least twice as much calcium as phosphorus. Now, this does not mean you need to study botany or chemistry in order to feed your iguana properly. If you follow the guidelines spelled out in this chapter, you will be feeding your iguana a diet with more than adequate amounts of calcium. As often as is possible, vegetables with particularly good or particularly bad calcium to phosphorus ratios will be noted as such.

Something to remember is that all the calcium in the world will do your iguana no good if it isn't getting enough vitamin D. In iguanas and most other animals, vitamin D regulates the absorption of calcium from the digestive tract. If there isn't enough vitamin D, any calcium the iguana ingests will just pass right through without being taken in and used by its body. There is considerable debate as to whether or not iguanas can absorb vitamin D from their food. If vitamin D doesn't come from the food, where does it come from? If you already read the section on lighting, you know that vitamin D is made in the iguana's skin when it is exposed to ultraviolet light. Be sure to read that section and follow the guidelines given there to be sure your iguana is busy making vitamin D when it basks under its lights. With iguanas—and many other reptiles—lighting and nutrition go hand-in-hand.

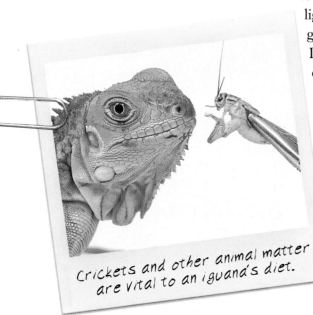

Crickets and other animal matter are vital to an iguana's diet.

The Protein Question

It was once believed that baby iguanas started out as insectivores or omnivores and gradually became herbivores as they matured. Research findings from the late 1980s through the present have confirmed that iguanas are herbivores their entire lives. However, there has been little research performed on just how much protein they need to have in their diets. The question of how much protein to feed pet iguanas is probably the most controversial one among owners, herpetologists, and veterinarians.

Part 3

Current thinking on this issue is that iguanas need little protein and that a varied, vegetarian diet like the one recommended in this book will supply your green friend with all the protein he needs. However, some recent studies show that baby and juvenile iguanas do require higher protein levels than adults. This does not mean that baby iguanas should be fed crickets or dog food, but it does mean that you need to include some vegetable sources of protein in the diet, especially for babies.

Can you feed your iguana too much protein? Absolutely. An iguana's entire physiology has adapted to live on a diet of plant matter, which is generally low in protein. Feeding an iguana a diet high in protein will lead to health problems. These problems show up gradually, and up until the iguana is very sick, he may appear fat and healthy to its owner. Some of the problems that seem to be caused by excess dietary protein are kidney and bladder stones, gout (crystals of uric acid that form in the joints and internal organs causing pain, inflammation, and loss of function in these areas), and mineralization of various tissues. Additionally, excess protein may interfere with the absorption of calcium, possibly causing a calcium deficiency. Protein from animal sources (such as meat, mice, and insects) seems to be more likely to cause these problems than protein from vegetable sources (such as beans, grains, and tofu).

Remember: iguanas do not need a lot of protein. In fact, it is dangerous to feed them large quantities of protein. Never feed your iguana any animal protein.

Dietary Diversity

Along with feeding your iguana the most nutritious vegetables, it is important to feed a variety of vegetables. This serves several functions. First of all, it will help stimulate appetite. No person wants to eat the same few foods all the time, and no iguana does either. Additionally, it is closer to what an iguana would experience in the wild. In the rainforest habitat of an iguana, there are thousands of species of plants that an iguana might

Mixed greens and other vegetables are often dietary staples for the green iguana.

consume, so it makes sense to include as many types as possible in captivity. Feeding your iguana a wide variety provides it with many different phytonutrients (chemicals plants contain that are not essential in the diet but do seem to provide some health benefits; the cancer-fighting lycopenes in tomatoes are one example), which are attracting a lot of interest in the human nutritionist community at the moment. Lastly—and perhaps most importantly—by including a wide variety of vegetables in the diet you minimize the possibility that the amount of any nutrient is too low. Feeding the most diverse foodstuffs you can helps ensure that your iguana will not lack any nutrients in his diet.

An iguana's diet can be broken down to a few major components: greens, other vegetables, fruits, and other items. We'll look at each component in detail. In each section, there will be a number of examples of specific items that can be fed to an iguana, and we'll note which ones are the best. Keep in mind that iguana nutrition is not an exact science, and future studies may result in changes as to what types of plants are good or bad for these lizards.

Greens

In nature, iguanas primarily eat the leaves of trees, vines, and shrubs. The closest things humans can offer to their scaly friends are leafy green vegetables. Leafy green vegetables should make up the majority of the diet, roughly half to two-thirds of the total amount of food offered.

Many types of greens are suitable for the green iguana's diet, so be sure to use as many as possible.

A list of leafy greens would include spinach, chard, collards, mustard greens, beet greens, bok choy, cabbage, broccoli, turnip greens, carrot tops, parsley, cilantro, lettuce, arugula, endive, escarole, dandelion greens, leeks, scallions, kale, watercress, and many others. Most grocery stores will carry at least a few of these plants. Some of the plants on this list are great for iguanas, and others are problematic for one reason or another. The problematic varieties can still be included in the diet, just in small quantities. These will be discussed later on in this section.

Out of the aforementioned plants, the best ones to offer seem to be collard greens, mustard greens, dandelion greens (the flowers are excellent to feed, as well), and turnip tops. At least one of these should be included in every meal and should be a substantial portion of the meal. All of these have excellent calcium to phosphorus ratios, as well as being high in many other vitamins and minerals. Almost as good as these best varieties are carrot tops, escarole, leeks, scallions, and celery leaves. These vegetables can also make up a significant portion of the diet.

Questionable Greens

Some greens lack nutrients, have a poor ration of calcium to phosphorus, or contain chemicals, which may be detrimental to the health of your iguana. Most of these can be fed to your iguanas in small quantities for variety but must not become a significant portion of the diet.

One category of greens and other vegetables that may cause problems is vegetables in the cabbage family. These include cabbage, kale, bok choy, Chinese cabbage, broccoli, Brussels sprouts, broccoli rabe, and cauliflower. All of these plants contain chemicals called goitrogens. Goitrogens interfere with the absorption of iodine by the digestive tract. Eventually, the lack of iodine will cause goiter (abnormal swelling of the thyroid gland), which is how these substances got their name. There is some debate about whether or not kale is as problematic as the other crucifers. A number of iguana owners have claimed that they have fed their iguanas large quantities of kale without any known deleterious effects. For now, however, research would suggest considering kale and the related vegetables as items to feed to your iguana only occasionally.

Another category of greens that are best fed sparingly are those that contain high levels of chemicals known as oxalates or oxalic acids. Oxalates bind with calcium and prevent it from being absorbed by the gut. Spinach, chard, beet greens, beets, sorrel, and rhubarb have high levels of oxalic acids. Therefore, although these vegetables are rich in many nutrients, they should not be fed frequently. When feeding any of these items, it would be beneficial to include some very calcium-rich greens or a little bit of calcium supplement.

Part 3

Folivory

Iguanas are called herbivores because they eat plants. More correctly, they should be called folivores, animals that primarily eat leaves (foliage). The eating of foliage is called folivory.

The last category of problem greens is lettuce. Lettuces are low in most nutrients, including calcium. Iceberg lettuce is primarily water with little nutritional value. Other lettuces, such as romaine and Boston, are better but not among the best things to feed to your lizards. The various lettuces can be fed to your iguanas in *tiny* amounts or as emergency food but mostly they should be avoided. Iceberg lettuce is especially bad, as it has so little nutritional value but is loved by many iguanas. Oftentimes, iguanas will ignore all other foods and pig out on iceberg lettuce. Most people familiar with iguanas will have heard of these little "lettuce addicts" and "lettuce junkies." When an iguana becomes a "lettuce addict," he will stop eating all other vegetables except lettuce and may go days without eating if lettuce is withheld. These iguanas invariably are malnourished and suffer from a variety of ailments. Converting a "lettuce addict" over to a healthy diet is a long process, and some iguanas die of their dietary deficiencies before they make the switch. No matter how much your iguana may love lettuce, feed it *sparingly or not at all.*

Other Vegetables

Although greens are the best items to feed your iguana, your lizard needs more variety than they can provide. This is where other vegetables come in. These items should make up about one-quarter to one-third of the total diet.

Almost any plant thought of as a vegetable can be included in the diet of a green iguana. As with the greens, some are better than others. Some to consider feeding to your iguana are asparagus, carrots (shredded), sweet potatoes (also shredded), mushrooms, sprouts (alfalfa, clover, chives, etc.), bell peppers, peas, snow peas, celery, green beans, okra, radishes, squash, corn, pumpkin, zucchini, and cucumbers. Radishes and cucumbers are low in most nutrients, so they should be used only once in a while. Asparagus, corn, and the various kinds of sprouts are low in calcium, so they too are best served only on occasion. Sprouts, especially alfalfa, are high in vitamins, minerals, and protein, making them a good choice despite their poor calcium level. The sweet potato also is low in calcium, but it is rich in vitamin A, fiber, and some minerals, so it is a good item to include; just be sure to feed those high-calcium greens with it. All of the others are good food items for your ig, and one or two can be offered at each meal, remembering to rotate in different items regularly.

Fruits

Although the majority of iguanas relish them, most fruits are high in sugars and little else. They are best regarded as treats rather than as staple foods. I generally include one small piece of some type of fruit in the food bowl each day. This seems to encourage my iguanas to come to the bowl and eat. Iguanas respond to color, and some bright reds and yellows in the food dish attract their attention. Just do not overdo it.

As much as your iguanas may love fruits, remember that they are almost the equivalent of candy. You wouldn't feed a human child a meal composed mostly of candy, nor should you feed your iguana meals composed mostly of fruits. Fruits are generally low in calcium, vitamins, and minerals. The high level of sugars in fruit can disrupt an iguana's complex digestive system. Too much sugar in the gut can cause problems, such as bloat (which in turn can lead to abnormal twisting of the digestive tract, known as torsion), diarrhea, and acidosis (high levels of acids in the bloodstream).

Fruits, especially citrus fruits, should be offered to iguanas in moderation.

A few fruits that are high in some vitamins and minerals are kiwis, figs, mangos, papayas, raspberries, and melons. Figs, papayas, and raspberries are especially good fruits to feed, as they are relatively high in calcium. It does no harm to offer other fruits on occasion, including bananas, apples, strawberries, blueberries, cherries, peaches, grapes, and others. Acidic fruits, such as pineapples, tomatoes, oranges, lemons, and others, are usually rejected by iguanas. However, if your iguana eats them, they will cause no harm to it in small quantities. Some owners have noticed that feeding acidic fruit to their iguanas results in runny, smelly feces–you have been warned!

Be sure to remove seeds, pits, and stems from any fruits you offer. They could cause choking or a blockage of the digestive tract.

Other Items

There are a number of other items that can be fed to iguanas on occasion. These items should be thought of as treats or supplements and not be given frequently. While most of them are not bad for your iguana, they are usually lacking in some nutrients or are too high in protein.

Various flowers can also be used to supplement the diet of captive green iguanas.

Various grain-based foods can be included in the diet once in a while. Some examples are pasta, whole-grain bread, and cooked grains, such as brown rice, wild rice, quinoa, oatmeal, wheat bulgur, and millet. These items are low in calcium and high in protein, but they are rich in several vitamins and, in most cases, iron. My iguanas are crazy about bread and will leap up to grab some. I actually have to throw it in the cage to avoid being bitten in their frenzy to eat the bread. These grain-based foods are helpful to offer if your iguana is suffering from diarrhea.

Legumes—meaning peas, beans, and lentils—and tofu (fermented soybean curd) make an occasional healthy snack for your iguana. These items are similar to the grains in being high in protein and low in calcium. Beans and lentils should be cooked and cooled before offering them to your iguana. Beans and seeds can also be soaked and sprouted as a way of offering protein and other nutrients. To make sure your iguana is getting adequate protein, offer one of these items in one or two feedings per month. When feeding iguanas younger than two years of age, include sources of vegetable protein once or twice per week.

Frozen vegetables can be used from time to time, but it is best if the vast majority of your iguana's diet is comprised of fresh vegetables. Remember that the process of freezing foods does destroy some of the vitamins, so fresh is always better. Also, some iguanas find frozen veggies less palatable than fresh. I find it handy to keep frozen corn and frozen peas on hand to add a little variety and provide the necessary protein. I also keep a box of frozen greens (usually turnip greens, but it varies) to use as an emergency food, such as when I can't get to the store, something went bad unexpectedly, or I overslept. I make sure frozen veggies are not used more than once or twice a month.

When you feed your iguana frozen vegetables, make sure they are fully thawed before you offer them. It is easiest to do this by using the microwave, which unfortunately might cause some further breakdown of vitamins. Usually, a small quantity of veggies is thawed in about one minute, but microwaves do vary. Do not give hot food to an iguana! Serious burns of the tongue, esophagus, and other parts of the digestive tract may result.

Commercial Diets

If you browse the reptile section of pet stores, you will probably notice at least one if not several varieties of prepackaged iguana foods for sale. It may be tempting to just give your iguana one of these diets, but current thinking on iguana nutrition is that this is a bad idea. Most of the diets are too high in protein and too low in calcium (and in some brands the calcium is not in a digestible form) and some other minerals. This is not to say that there are no good commercial diets available, just that most are not suitable for use as the only source of nutrition. Apparently, the iguanas farmed in Central America are fed a prepared diet almost exclusively, but to my knowledge this diet is not available to the general hobbyist.

If you decide to use a commercial diet, I would suggest that it make up no more than ten percent of the total diet. This way you can be sure your iguana is still getting enough calcium and not too much protein. Choose a commercial diet that has no animal ingredients but has high fiber, a good calcium-to-phosphorus ratio, and a protein content of no higher than 25 percent. The pelleted and meal-type diets seem to be better than the canned ones. You can also use commercial diets as treats or as emergency foods.

Supplements

If offered a complete and varied diet, an iguana will need supplements only occasionally, if at all. Some owners claim a properly fed iguana does not need supplements; they have kept iguanas healthy for years without using them. Research on iguana diets does not provide a clear picture as to the necessity of supplements. Reptile veterinarians see iguanas in their offices suffering from both dietary deficiencies and toxically high levels of vitamins and minerals. However, most iguanas that have nutritional problems have deficiencies, not excessive vitamin levels. It seems more prudent to provide some supplementation, but be careful not to overdo it.

For an adult, I recommend giving a high-quality vitamin/mineral/calcium supplement once every two weeks. Increase to once weekly for an actively breeding female. Hatchlings also should be given supplements in their diets once a week, with perhaps a pinch of extra calcium given another time weekly. This regimen has worked well for my iguanas for the past 12 years. When using a powdered supplement (which is the type I recommend), only lightly dust the food with it. You should only be using about enough supplement to cover a fingernail (about equivalent to one-eighth of a teaspoon).

There are many different supplements on the market, making it difficult to choose a good one. There are several things to look for in a supplement, as well as a few things to avoid. First, avoid any supplement not made specifically for reptiles. Supplements for birds, fish, or other animals will do no good and may harm iguanas and other reptiles.

Among the various reptile supplements, I would recommend a powdered vitamin. Liquid vitamins tend to spoil quickly and often are not accepted by iguanas. Vitamins that are meant to be added to drinking water are not a good choice either. Iguanas don't drink all that often, and putting vitamins in drinking water just encourages bacterial growth. A powdered vitamin that is made to be added to the food is the best way to go.

So, we've now narrowed down the search several levels. Next you need to look at the ingredients and the analysis on the label. Avoid any vitamins with conspicuous animal ingredients; remember that these are vegetarian animals. If possible, find a vitamin supplement that does not contain minerals, because when combined, the minerals speed the breakdown of the vitamins. Admittedly, these are hard to find in many pet stores. If you buy a vitamin supplement that does contain minerals, look for vitamins with at least twice the amount of calcium as phosphorus. Also, look for one that contains most of its vitamin A in the form of beta carotene. This negates any chance of giving your iguana too much vitamin A. Beta carotene is transformed into vitamin A by the body. If your iguana has enough vitamin A, its body just excretes the beta carotene. Once you've screened down the selection of vitamins this far, pick the one that has the most complete list of vitamins and minerals.

You should also get a calcium supplement. Again, pick one that is made for reptiles. Some calcium supplements have rather high levels of phosphorus; these should be avoided. Vitamin D is added to many of the calcium supplements on the market. This is of no consequence to iguana owners because iguanas do not appear to be able to absorb vitamin D through their digestive tract. So, while a supplement that contains vitamin D will do no harm, it is not necessary. Just buy a calcium supplement that has no or low levels of phosphorus.

Feeding Your Iguana

Now that you've just read all the bits about what to feed and what not to feed your iguana, you need to know *how* to feed him. There is nothing really complicated about this, but there are some things to do and some things to not do. We'll be talking about the feeding schedule, food preparation, and a few minor points.

Preparation

If you are familiar with reptiles, you may have noticed that they don't really chew their food. Iguanas are no exception. For the most part, they chomp off pieces of leaves and swallow. This lack of chewing does present a choking hazard, although wild iguanas do not seem to suffocate in any numbers. Still, it is best to chop or shred all the food items into bite-sized pieces. Leafy greens can be torn and the other vegetables and fruits chopped. Hard vegetables, such as carrots, sweet potatoes, and beets, should be grated before offering them. Alternatively, you could lightly steam the hard vegetables, let them cool, and then chop them into small chunks.

Aside from helping prevent your iguana from choking, chopping up the food allows you to thoroughly mix it. Mixing the food keeps your iguana from separating out the items he prefers and leaving the other items. While it is nice to feed your iguana the food he likes, this can lead to nutritional problems. After all, a child left to his or her own preferences would be likely to eat little besides cakes and candies. Your iguana is no different.

Presented with an abundance of food and the ability to select the items he likes, he will do so, usually selecting the bits of colorful fruits and vegetables and leaving most of the nutritious greens behind. Chopping and mixing stops most of this. If you have a really picky iguana or one that is particularly adroit at sifting out only what he wants to eat, you can put all the food items into a food processor and make a thick sludge out of them. This may look unpalatable to you, but most iguanas will eat it without much fuss.

For a really picky eater, one that does not like certain nutritious foods or likes one food to the exclusion of others, you can slowly bring him

Iguanas will relish a well-prepared bowl of salad.

around to eating more variety. To do this, offer mixes mostly of the food item or items your ig likes, adding a tiny bit of the food item he won't eat. As the days go by, gradually increase the proportion of the disliked item. Soon you will find your iguana accepts that item without a problem. If you want or need to do this with more than one item, you will have the most success if you try to coax your iguana to eat only one of the items at a time. If you try to hide more than one unwanted item in the food bowl, your iguana will likely catch on and reject the entire dish.

Schedule

It is common to hear people say that reptiles have a slow metabolism and do not need to be fed every day. I've heard it recommended that you feed iguanas three times a week, every other day, and on other similar schedules. I think that these incorrect ideas come from those familiar with snakes and who extend their knowledge to other reptiles they know less about.

While it is true that a healthy, well-fed iguana can go a day or even several days without eating, their biology is geared toward having food every day. After all, for the most part, they live in places that have an abundance of plant life. When you are a browsing animal, you do not have an unsuccessful hunt. In the wild, iguanas normally eat every day; they should have the opportunity to do likewise in captivity. Your iguana might on occasion skip eating for a day or so, but you should offer food daily anyway.

Even though they are consumed with gusto, bananas should be offered only once or twice a week.

Iguanas seem to eat best in the morning, but I've found them to be adaptable to your schedule. One thing to avoid is feeding them at night or close to the time you shut the lights off on their enclosures. As you know, iguanas are diurnal animals, and they will not feed at night. This means that if you feed your iguana at night, the food will sit until the next morning, possibly becoming rotten and unhealthy to eat. It certainly will be less palatable than fresh food.

If you feed your iguana late in the day, within

roughly the last hour before you turn off the enclosure lighting, he may have insufficient warmth to properly digest his food. This can lead to the food spoiling in the digestive tract, which can cause serious problems. Feed your iguana so that he has plenty of time to get digestion underway before his enclosure cools down for the night. Because iguanas seem to prefer to eat in the morning, this would be the ideal time to feed your ig.

No matter what time of day you feed your iguana, you should try to stick to a regular feeding schedule. You'll find your iguana will get very attached to this routine. Mine even act up on days that I feed them late or skip feeding: they throw their food bowls (including uneaten food) all over the cage.

When you feed your iguana each day, you should remove any uneaten food and give the food bowl a thorough wash in hot soapy water.

Presentation

This section is not about making your iguana's food bowl look like a creation on the pages of *Fine Dining* or other gourmet publications. Rather, it is about how to actually give your iguana his food.

Your iguana's food should be placed in a bowl or on a plate that is sturdy enough to not be broken when the iguana accidentally flings it across the cage or jumps down on it from his perch. Any bowl made of porcelain or glass is out. The unbreakable plastic bowls sold for large dogs work well, as do stainless steel bowls. The large, heavy crockery bowls sold for small animals and reptiles can be good choices if you buy one large and heavy enough.

Placing the food in a bowl prevents the substrate from getting into the food, which can cause several problems, including choking, impaction, and bacterial infection. Some keepers use a paper plate or butcher's paper for feeding. This eliminates the need to clean the bowl, but it is

Carrots and other brightly-colored vegetables should be included in your iguana's diet.

This intermediate-sized iguana will eat several times a day if permitted.

far from an attractive option. It also increases the chance that your iguana will walk through his food, creating more opportunities for bacterial growth.

I recommend putting the food bowl on the bottom of the cage rather than up on one of the perches. This prevents your iguana from knocking the bowl down and spilling his food all over the cage. Also, this stimulates your iguana to be a little more active, as he now has to climb down to eat and back up to get to the heating and lighting.

Some iguanas can get very pushy at feeding time. My male will leap at the hand holding the bowl or attempt to climb up my leg if I'm not careful. Just be aware of this and keep yourself from being accidentally harmed by your eager iguana. You may also want to warn a pet-sitter.

Amount

Many new iguana owners are clueless about how much to feed their iguanas. Some books do not address this topic, and pet store help can be terribly vague about this subject.

The problem with addressing the issue of how much to feed an iguana is that–like people–iguanas vary greatly in the amount of food they will consume. Add to this that each iguana will have days when it eats more or less food than normal, and that the amount an individual iguana eats will change with age. Therefore, any recommendations on the amount to feed igs are just that–recommendations. Adjust your quantities by what your individual iguana needs. You should be able to figure out the right amount within the first month to six weeks of owning your scaly friend.

A baby iguana needs somewhere between three and six tablespoons of coarsely chopped food per day. Adjust this upward as the iguana grows until you reach roughly three cups of food for a full-grown adult.

It is better to feed your iguana too much than too little. It's okay if there are some leftovers. If your iguana consumes all of his food in a minute or so, then you probably should be

Gardening for Your Iguana

If you enjoy gardening as a hobby as I do, there's no reason you cannot combine your love of your iguana with your love of gardening. During the warmer months, you can grow a sizable proportion of your iguana's food yourself, providing your pet with produce of unparalleled freshness. Also, if you garden organically, you remove any risk posed by pesticides and such. Unfortunately, space considerations prevent me from discussing how to grow these plants, but your local library and bookstores will have a good selection of gardening references.

Any of the foods mentioned in the main feeding section can be grown in your garden as iguana food. Here I'll mention some iguana foods that you usually won't find in your produce department but could grow in your garden, yard, or indoor pots. As with the iguana food you can buy in your produce department, some of the plants mentioned here are better to feed to your iguana than others. In many cases, the nutritional value of the plants is unknown. Because many of them aren't typically used as human or animal food, there has been little research on their nutritional value.

Alfalfa: This is a relative of the beans that does well in poor soils. It has deep roots that pull nutrients up from below the topsoil. It is an excellent source of calcium, protein, fiber, and trace minerals.

Bean leaves: The leaves and flowers of bean plants are edible and make for good variety in your iguana's diet.

Clover: This plant grows wild in many yards. The leaves and flowers are good sources of several vitamins.

Grape leaves: Despite having been used as a human food for thousands of years, nutritional information on grape leaves is elusive. Some claim that they are high in oxalates, making them unsuitable as a staple iguana food but great as an occasional treat.

Hibiscus: Unless you live in the warmer areas of the country, you'll want to grow your hibiscus in large pots; they are not cold-hearty. The leaves and flowers are high in calcium and other nutrients.

Mints: The many varieties of mints are all easy to grow and reasonably nutritious. They also contain chemicals that fight infections. Use them as treats.

Mulberry: The leaves of mulberry trees are one of the best sources of calcium available, and the fruits are high in the mineral as well.

Nasturtiums: The flowers and leaves are wonderful sources of calcium and other nutrients. They are easy to grow and will do well in pots if you are cramped for space.

Pea leaves and flowers: This is a great plant to include in the garden as it offers three different foods for your iguana: leaves, flowers, and pods. The leaves are decent sources of calcium and protein.

Raspberry leaves: Iguanas seem to love these, but there is little information on their nutritional value. They may be high in oxalates, so use them for variety.

Rose of Sharon: A close relative of the hibiscus but tolerant of cold weather, this plant is probably similar in nutritional value to hibiscus.

Roses: This is another plant that provides multiple iguana foods. Your ig can eat the leaves, flowers, and fruits. The fruits are high in vitamin C, while the nutritional values of the other plant parts are not known.

Part 3

feeding more. Don't forget to look at the overall size of your ig. If he is extremely round and sausage-like, you need to cut back on the food. If he is thin with a bony look, start feeding him more.

Water

Hopefully, it does not come as a surprise that your iguana needs water to drink. Some iguana books state that iguanas do not drink often and that frequent drinking is a sign of illness. I have found that iguanas do drink on a fairly regular basis, and therefore, they should have clean, fresh water available at all times.

As with the food, a sturdy dish is highly recommended. You also want a heavy one. Trust me–you really don't want to have to re-clean your freshly cleaned cage because your iguana spilled his water. Large, heavy crockery dishes make great water bowls because they are so heavy. It does make them a bit of a chore to take out of the cage and clean, but it's worth it to not have to deal with a sopping-wet cage every day. Weighted plastic dog bowls may make a good alternative, but I have no experience with them. They would certainly be worth trying.

Each day, you should remove the water bowl from the cage, dump the water, and replace it with fresh water. Once a week, soak the bowl in about one part bleach to four parts water for 15 minutes and then rinse it thoroughly. This will keep the bowl relatively free of germs.

Most iguanas have a tendency to defecate in the water bowl. While this behavior may seem disgusting to humans, let's look at it from the iguana's point of view. In the wild, iguanas tend to live in the trees overhanging streams, rivers, and lakes. When nature calls, an iguana positions himself over the edge of the branch and does his business. The waste falls in the water, and the current carries it away. In captivity, the water bowl is the closest substitute to a river the iguana has. It doesn't have the brain capacity to realize that there is no current to carry the waste away; you have to be the current. If your iguana does go in its bowl, you should clean the bowl immediately, soaking it in a bleach and water solution for at least 15 minutes before rinsing, filling, and returning it to the cage.

Part Four
Long-Term Care and Husbandry

"Now that bob is getting into old age, I decided it was time to buy him a little wheelchair and install a safety rail on his climbing log."

Living With an Iguana

As the title suggests, this chapter is about living with your iguana. I do not mean having an iguana in a cage and just looking at him—I mean turning your iguana into a real pet. This will mean letting him out of his cage, handling him frequently, trimming his claws, and being nice to him.

Adjustment Period

When you first get your iguana, he will not know the difference between you and a predator. With patience and persistence, you will win him over. The key is to go slowly, following his lead.

Once you've had your iguana for a few days, you should start getting him accustomed to you and

If well cared for, iguanas can be long-lived creatures.

your habits. Talk to him when you feed him and clean the cage so he gets used to your voice. You can even just talk to him when you are in the same room.

Sometimes you may want to put your hands in the cage for no reason other than to get him used to you. Just stick a hand in there and keep it fairly still. You can talk to him at this time. Your iguana will probably run away at first and may do this for the first several times you put your hands in. Eventually, he may become curious and come out to flick your hand with his tongue. That's a good sign.

After a day or two talking to him and getting him used to the presence of your hands, you are ready to move on to handling him.

Handling and Holding

It is a bad idea to start handling your iguana by quickly grabbing him and lifting him out of the cage. He will think he has just been snatched up by some bird and is about to become a meal. His adrenaline will be flowing, and he'll be primed to fight or escape. This is not the mindset you want your iguana in when trying to establish a fulfilling pet-keeper relationship.

You must go slowly and patiently. Approach your iguana from the front or from where he can see you. Speak softly and gently. Place your hand under your iguana and gently lift.

He will almost certainly try to run away. Remember that being handled is a foreign experience for a wild animal. Do not be discouraged.

Usually only those iguanas that have been raised from juveniles will be able to be completely trusted on their owner's shoulder while outdoors.

When he runs away, do not chase him madly about the cage. This will only stress him out further, and the ig will associate the appearance of your hand with being chased. Stay motionless and wait until he calms down. Continue to speak to him with a soft voice. Once he has calmed, put your hand under him and lift him again. Repeat this process several times until you can lift him without

Part 4

MY Iguana Bit Me!

Iguana owners will be bitten by their iguana eventually. It goes with the territory. Hopefully, you will be bitten by a young iguana and not a full-grown adult.

The first thing to do when bitten is to remain calm. Most of the time, iguana bites do not require medical attention. You will need to wash out the wound using an antiseptic, such as povidone-iodine. After the wound is clean, dab on a little antibiotic ointment and cover with a bandage. If the bleeding doesn't stop in a reasonable amount of time, you may need stitches.

Large iguanas can produce horrific bites. These almost always occur when the iguana is not tame, the owner ignored warning signs, or if the iguana is a male in breeding condition. If you are bitten by a large iguana, you probably should seek medical attention. It is better to go to the emergency room and find out that you didn't need to than to need emergency care and not receive it.

If your iguana bites and holds on, don't try to pry him off. You could injure your iguana or make the wound you have even worse. I've had good results running a latched-on reptile (iguanas, pythons, and others) under cold water. They generally let go in a few seconds.

Remember that an iguana does not bite out of meanness or evil. It is a wild animal with limited faculties to make sense of the world around it. Iguanas bite mainly because they are afraid or feel threatened.

freaking him out. It will take several sessions over the course of a few days.

At this time, be cautious about taking him out of the cage. Everything around him is still new and scary. He is liable to bolt if there are strange noises, fast movements, the appearance of other humans or pets, or for no reason you can fathom. Be prepared for him to jump and be ready to restrain him–gently but firmly. Remember that your iguana will lose his tail if you grab it, so avoid doing that. You can also handle him only in his cage at first, as this minimizes the chance of escape.

When he is used to being picked up, you now want to start handling him frequently. Don't overdo it, but a 15-minute session of handling once or twice a day is a good start. If your iguana gets too freaky, cut the duration a bit. Keep at it. Iguanas will only become nice pets if you handle them frequently. In a week or two, your iguana will be ready to be handled for longer periods of time. Increase the duration of handling sessions to 30 minutes. When your iguana gets used to that, increase to 45 minutes or an hour. After you hit the hour mark, your iguana has definitely become used to you, and you can be more liberal about handling him when you want. Just be sure to handle your ig every day of his life, so that he stays tame as he grows. Igs seem to prefer set schedules, so try to arrange your handling sessions to be near the same time each day.

During the handling sessions, handle your iguana for the entire time, even if he squirms and struggles. You need to show your iguana not only that you are the one in control but also that his struggles won't do any good. Once he realizes that you mean him no harm and that struggling doesn't work, he should calm down and tolerate handling.

Be sure to support your iguana completely when holding him. If he feels like he's going to fall, he will dig his sharp, little claws deep into your flesh. This can cause you to jump and possibly fling your poor iguana through the air. This will not help you socialize him.

For a baby or small juvenile, you should let his body rest in the palm of your hand. This will provide your iguana with a sense of support and security.

For a larger iguana, you should let his body rest on the length of your forearm with his tail sticking out under your arm behind you. Again, support as much of the iguana's body as you can. If you have a very large iguana, you may have to use two hands. Let most of the body rest on your forearm and use your other hand to hold his chest. Do not hold him by his neck or head. You can also hold a large ig on your chest with his head resting on your shoulder.

Socializing (Taming)

Getting your iguana accustomed to handling is the first step on the road to having a friendly and affectionate pet iguana. Now that you have started off this relationship on the right foot, you need to foster it along.

Trust

As you continue in your daily interactions with your iguana, you must not give him reason to believe you will do him harm. Avoid moving rapidly, using a loud voice, or anything else that will startle your iguana. When you are in the early stages of building a relationship with your iguana, these behaviors can cause him to regress a bit.

Remember that your iguana does not understand roughhousing or teasing. To him, these are aggressive interactions, and he will respond in kind. Iguanas do not become accustomed to these types of play. If you roughhouse with your iguana, he will never settle down into a good pet. *Never* hit your iguana to punish him. This is a serious breach of trust.

A good way to build some trust with your ig is to feed him by hand. You should not feed him his whole meal by hand, or he'll become used to this and start ignoring the food bowl. When you have your iguana out for some handling, feed him a few tasty morsels from your hand. Choose some item your ig likes and give him a few pieces of it when he's being handled. Just be careful that your ig doesn't get overly excited by

Albino iguanas are a relatively new novelty among reptile enthusiasts.

the treat. Kermit goes nuts for bread, so even though she loves it, it is not a good hand-feeding food; I'd likely get a bad bite. I use strawberry tops and hibiscus flowers as my preferred hand-foods. Edible flowers may be a good choice because so many iguanas love them and they are easy to hold in a way that keeps your hand away from your ig's teeth.

Petting Your Iguana

When your iguana is out of his cage for social time, you should try petting and lightly scratching him. Each iguana has his own preferences for how and where he wants to be petted. You'll pick up on your ig's preferences pretty quickly.

Pet your iguana only in the direction his scales point. Petting in the other direction annoys an iguana. Additionally, petting "against the grain" can abrade your skin.

Only pet an iguana's head after you are sure he trusts you. Otherwise, he may view the hand coming toward his head as a threat. Pay attention to his body language. Some iguanas simply do not like their heads touched. Respect that and pet your ig on his body, neck, or wherever else he seems to like it.

Time of the Month

Many people who work with iguanas have noticed that male iguanas often become aggressive to women who are menstruating. This can happen even if the male is not in breeding season, but it is most associated with males in breeding condition.

Why this occurs is not known. The theory is that menstruating women smell different to male iguanas, and the difference, for some reason, triggers aggression.

If you are a woman who owns a male iguana, you should be cautious around him when you are menstruating. If you are a man who owns a male iguana, warn any female household members about this possibility, so they can take precautions as needed.

Warning Signs

Although they cannot speak, iguanas often will try to tell you something. They do this with body language. An iguana who is done being petted will let you know through his posture, gestures, and such. If you ignore these clues, you will probably get bitten.

An irritated iguana may bob or shake his head, inflate his dewlap, hiss, or twitch his tail. Some iguanas will smack at an annoyance–like someone petting them incorrectly–with a forelimb. This is Kermit's favorite gesture of irritation. Standing up high on their legs is also an expression of anger.

An iguana will often puff up with air when ticked off. This often is followed by a hiss. An iguana performing this behavior is really irritated or angry, and open-mouth gaping may follow. Biting is surely next.

When your iguana performs these behaviors, be on your guard. If it seems related to handling or petting, you should probably stop doing that and let your ig calm down for a bit.

Happy Signs

An iguana also has signs that he's contented. Generally this involves a relaxed posture. Closing both eyes while being petted is a sure sign of contentment (closing one eye is avoidance behavior).

A single bob of the head when your ig first sees you is a greeting behavior. It is like saying, "I see you!"

Relaxed and content iguanas show bright colors. They darken in reaction to stress.

Together Time

The more time you invest in interacting with your iguana, the better a pet he will become. Although he needs to be in his enclosure where it is warm and humid enough for him, you should make having him out for an hour or two of social time each day a priority. You can use heating pads or additional heat lamps to keep your iguana warm enough when he's not in his cage. There's also body heat–iguanas will cuddle for warmth.

Create times for you and your iguana to be together. This could be lying on the couch together in front of the TV, having him on your lap or on back of the monitor while you check email, or anything else that gets you and your iguana spending time together. You could let your iguana out to roam while you do your morning routine–just remember that he's underfoot.

Taking your iguana along when visiting a friend is fine, as long as your friend approves. Take along a portable litter pan, a water bowl, and some food. Bring your iguana in a carrier, and put him in there if he acts up. Remember that while he's out visiting, your iguana probably will not be at the proper temperature. Limit such visits to less than two hours and put him right into the cage when you get home.

Going for walks and sitting out on the deck with your iguana are fine, but there are a number of precautions you must take before bringing your iguana outdoors. Check the chapter on outdoor iguanas for details.

Grooming

Because an iguana does not have fur, it may seem strange to talk about grooming them. However, there are some parts of iguana care that fall under this category. No, you won't be taking your iguana into the salon for a shampoo, but you will be trimming his claws and possibly helping him shed.

Claw-Trimming

Iguanas in captivity do not wear down their claws nearly as much as they would in nature. In fact, you may think your iguana has razors attached to his

Bleeding Claws

While trimming your iguana's claws, you may eventually cut too much off a claw and cause bleeding. Don't panic; just act swiftly to curtail the bleeding.

I highly recommend having some type of blood coagulating agent, a styptic powder or styptic stick, on hand when you trim your iguana's nails. These products are available at pet stores and pharmacies. They stop blood flow quickly.

When you get a bleeding claw, pack the area with the powder as directed. The nail should stop bleeding soon. For the next few days keep an eye on the claw for any sign of infection. I put a little antibiotic ointment on the claw after it stops bleeding as an additional precaution against infection.

Soaking Softens Claws

To make trimming the claws go a bit more smoothly, do it after your iguana has had his weekly soaking. Thirty minutes or so in the warm water will soften the claws and make them easier to trim. The soaking will also help prevent your ig from defecating during the claw-trimming.

feet instead of claws. If you do not trim them, you will find each session of handling your iguana a painful and probably bloody experience.

Although most keepers are nervous about trimming their ig's claws, it really is a simple procedure. The more times you do it, the more confident you'll become. Needless to say, claw trimming is much easier when your iguana is tame. The first few times you trim his claws, your ig may get jumpy, but he'll get used to it after a few times.

To start with, you should trim your iguana's claws in a quiet place. A place that your iguana feels comfortable and secure is ideal. It is important that the place you choose has good lighting; you need to see what you are doing.

You will need to have a good set of claw clippers. I've found the two best types to be human toenail clippers and the clippers sold specifically for reptiles. Avoid the ones for birds, as these hold the claw in place and can cause an accident if your iguana jerks away.

Trim off only the very tip of the claw. You want to avoid hitting the quick (the living part, including a blood vessel, toward the base and extending into the surrounding dead claw tissue) and making your iguana bleed. This also hurts, which could make your iguana bite or fuss the next time you trim his claws. Also, you want to leave your iguana with claws for climbing, so just take off the narrow tip.

How often you need to trim your iguana's claws varies with the individual, age, and housing situation. Young iguanas that are growing rapidly need their claws trimmed more often than do adults. If there are many rough surfaces (limbs and rocks) in your ig's enclosure, you'll need to do less frequent trimming, as his claws will be getting extra wear.

You can also have a veterinarian show you how to trim your ig's nails. Be sure you go to a vet who has experience with iguanas, not just cats, dogs, or birds. See the veterinary chapter for information on how to find a vet.

Shedding

For the most part, your iguana will shed his skin by himself without your help. Sometimes, however, some skin is stubborn and sticks to certain areas. That's when you need to intervene.

It is better to prevent shedding problems rather than to correct them after they happen. To prevent them, keep your ig's cage at the proper humidity and give him his weekly soak. When you notice that he's begun shedding, spray the cage an extra time or two each day until he's done.

Regular baths and good grooming practices can help your iguana's shedding process.

The most common areas where shed skin remains stuck are the toes, the dorsal spines, and the tail tip. When you handle and examine your iguana, look for bits of old skin in these areas. Unshed skin will look gray and probably dried out.

If you find unshed skin in these areas, you should remove it. Try to nudge it off with a finger. If it refuses to budge, you can gently use your fingernail to pick it off. It may still be stuck, in which case you need to try more dramatic measures.

Soak your iguana for 30 minutes or so. Leave him in the water and while he's there, start to pick at the shed with your fingers. Be gentle; you don't want to scratch his skin.

If the skin still refuses to come off, dab the area with some cooking oil. Do this two or three times a day for a couple of days. This should soften up the skin enough for easy removal.

When You Go Away

When you go on vacation or away for the weekend, you have to make sure your iguana will get adequate care while you are gone. This may mean getting a sitter or boarding your ig.

Getting a Sitter

I think getting a pet-sitter is better for your iguana than boarding. Your iguana gets to stay

Salmonella Reminder

Although you want your iguana to spend lots of time with you, remember not to let him up on kitchen counters or anywhere else he could pass salmonella along to you or your housemates.

Having your iguana out is not a good idea while you are preparing food. If you pick up your ig to move him somewhere and then handle the food, you could have just contaminated dinner.

Although many keepers let their iguana roam on the kitchen floor, I have a strict "no reptiles in the kitchen" rule.

If you let your iguana loose in the bathroom, remember to disinfect the tub and sink if he comes into contact with them.

in his comfortable home and not be subjected to the stress of new surroundings and new people. Also, because he won't be exposed to other animals, there is less chance that he'll contract a disease (this doesn't happen frequently when boarding an ig, but it could).

Ideally, your pet-sitter will be a friend or relative who doesn't mind coming over and caring for your ig while you're away. However, you may have to hire someone. To find a good pet-sitter, ask around at vet offices, pet stores, herp club meetings, and the local animal shelter. Those places can steer you toward reputable sitters. You can also look in the local paper or phonebook, but I prefer to get recommendations from a trustworthy source.

Once you have found a potential sitter, ask him or her for references. If he or she does not have them or doesn't give them to you, find someone else. When you are given references, check them. Call up at least two of the people listed as references and ask about their experience with the pet-sitter. If you like what you hear, then you probably have found a good sitter.

When anyone, whether it's your mom or a professional sitter, pet-sits for your ig, be sure to leave a complete and detailed list of the care they are to provide. It helps to break it down by day and by task. Leave a phone number or two where you can be contacted and leave the number for your regular vet. Show the sitter where you keep the food, spray bottles, first aid supplies, and anything else they might need. Make sure the sitter is clear on when he or she is expected to be there. Good sitters are worth their weight in gold. When you find one, it never hurts to tip him or her well.

Boarding Your Iguana

If you cannot find a sitter, you will have to find some place to board your green friend. Many cat and dog kennels will not take iguanas for boarding, but some will. However, I would rather take my iguana to a place that is more familiar with reptiles and/or iguanas.

Part 4

Some pet stores and vet offices provide boarding services. If you are lucky, your regular vet boards iguanas. If not, you will need to look elsewhere. Ask your vet or other knowledgeable people for a recommendation.

Once you find a place that accepts iguanas, ask to come for a tour. You want to make sure the place is clean and that they have sufficient facilities to care for an iguana. During your tour, you can ask some questions to find out how much the staff knows about iguanas. Try to be pleasant and nonconfrontational when you do this.

If they are going to house your iguana in a steel cage with an open front door, think twice about boarding your ig at that facility. This type of cage is very hard to heat adequately, and it does not retain sufficient humidity.

If you have a local herp society, you can check with them to see if a member would be willing to take in your iguana during your absence. It helps if you belong to the herp society in question or at least are on friendly terms with some of its members. Boarding at a friend's house is also a preferable option to boarding at a vet office or pet store.

Part 4

Medical Issues

It is a sad fact that most iguanas (and other exotic animals) do not receive proper veterinary care. Most owners will only take their iguana to a vet when he is already visibly and seriously ill. For these iguanas, the prognosis is not good. Reptiles–iguanas included–are experts at hiding illness until they are extremely sick. By that time, it may be too late for medical intervention. It is far better for your prized pet to receive the recommended checkups to detect problems before they become life threatening.

Iguanas should receive regular vet care. Additionally, they should receive whatever medical care they require as the need arises. If you cannot or will not provide necessary medical

Iguana owners need to understand and practice good husbandry techniques.

care to your iguana, please do not keep one. It is the moral obligation of every pet owner to provide his or her pets with proper medical care.

Finding an Iguana Vet

Finding a vet for reptiles is not as easy as finding a vet for a cat or dog, although with the increased popularity of keeping reptiles as pets, it is now easier to find one than ever before. However, there are vets who call themselves "exotic animal vets" or even "reptile vets" who do not have a lot of experience with reptiles or iguanas.

There are a number of places you can look. You can start by calling vets in the phonebook who list themselves as exotic animal or reptile vets. Ask to speak to the vet and then ask the vet exactly what experience he or she has with iguanas.

An excellent resource for finding herp vets is the Association of Reptilian and Amphibian Veterinarians. They could point you to an affiliated veterinarian in your area. You can find them on the web at www.arav.org.

Signs of Illness

It can be difficult to tell when your iguana is ill. Iguanas are adapted to hide illness as well as they can. In the wild, it is the sick and the weak that are most likely to fall victim to predators.

Here are some signs that your iguana should see a vet. However, the best way to know if your ig needs medical attention is by knowing what is normal for him. If you spend enough time observing him, you will know what is normal and what is not.

Your iguana is probably ill if:

1. He hasn't eaten in over three days and is not in breeding condition or too cold

2. There is a discharge from the nose, eye, mouth, or vent

3. He is limping or otherwise favoring a limb

4. He is listless or lethargic

5. The stools do not appear normal

6. He has any strange bumps, swellings, or discolorations

7. He appears weak

8. He trembles or twitches.

Your local animal shelters and pet stores are good places to check to find a vet for your iguana. They may have recommendations or even a vet they normally use. They may also have some anecdotes about various vets that could be interesting and informative. Local zoos and wildlife rehabilitators can also help point you to a good vet.

If you have a local herp society, this may be the best place to find a good iguana vet. The members of the club are sure to have experiences with many of the vets in your area and can steer you to the right one for you and your iguana.

Lastly, there is always the Internet. You can look on reptile lists and message boards for recommendations.

Once you have a recommendation or two, call the vets and see if you can have a short chat with them. Remember that veterinarians are busy folks; keep the chat short. You are just trying to determine what their iguana experience is and if you think that you and the vet will be a good match. When you find one you like, make an appointment.

The First Vet Visit

Ideally, you will take your iguana in for his first vet visit no more than a month after you get him. The sooner you get your ig into the vet after you purchase him, the more likely you are to catch any problems early on and get them taken care of before they become too serious. Also, some pet shops and other sellers guarantee their iguanas to be healthy for anywhere from a day to a week or more, but you must have a vet examine the animal during this timeframe.

At the first visit, the vet is likely to want a stool sample to look for internal parasites. Try to get one that morning. If your iguana is withholding, try giving him a soak, but take him out of the water before he goes. You don't want to take in a watery sample.

Regular check-ups are important for your green iguanas.

Part 4

The vet will examine your iguana, looking for signs of various diseases and external parasites. He may draw some blood to check the levels of various enzymes, hormones, and dissolved minerals.

At the end of the exam, find out about the vet's emergency policies and what to do during an emergency after hours. You should also ask if the vet boards iguanas or if they have some pet-sitters or boarding facilities they recommend for iguanas.

Checkups

After the first visit, you want to take your iguana in for regular checkups. Your iguana should see the vet once a year. These checkups are invaluable in catching an illness during its early stages, when the chance of successful treatment is highest.

Common Medical Problems

Most iguana medical problems are directly or indirectly caused by poor husbandry. If you take proper care of your iguana–including excellent housing, diet, lighting, and heating–he will be unlikely to become ill or injured. This cannot be stressed highly enough. However, the following are some of the most common medical problems iguanas can experience.

Abscesses are frequently encountered in green iguanas, especially in the tail and hindquarters.

Abscesses

Abscesses are unpleasant pockets of hardened pus that form under your iguana's skin. They are usually caused when bacteria enter a small wound. The wound heals up, but the bacteria are still inside. As the iguana's body attempts to fight the bacteria and the bacteria proliferate, pus and other materials build up. If untreated, the bacteria in the abscess can escape and spread, causing infections in other parts of the body.

On the outside, abscesses appear to be hard, semi-mobile lumps under your lizard's skin. They can get quite large. Your ig may become agitated if you touch the area; abscesses can be painful.

If you suspect your iguana has an abscess, you should seek veterinary care. The vet will slice open the abscess, clean out the pus and crud, and stitch up the wound. He or she will almost definitely prescribe antibiotics.

Kermit had a bout with abscesses several yeas ago. She got one, and I had it treated. Then she got another, and another. Finally, my vet discovered the cause in an X-ray: she had a small abscess in a vertebral bone. Bacteria were escaping from this abscess and causing the formation of others. He put Kermit on injectible antibiotics, and she's been abscess-free ever since.

Burns

Unfortunately, burns are one of the most common problems seen in iguanas. For the most part, they are totally preventable. Preventing burns means securely attaching your iguana's heat lamps and monitoring the other heating devices to be certain they are working correctly.

If your iguana gets a severe burn, you should take him to the vet. Burns are prone to infection, and bad ones will cause your ig to go into shock.

For a minor burn, first soak the area in cool water. Do this for at least 15 minutes. You can soak sterile pads in cool water and lay them gently over the burn if it is on a part of the body that is hard to soak. After soaking, lightly coat the burn with antibiotic ointment. Reapply the ointment the next day, but leave the burn open to the air afterward.

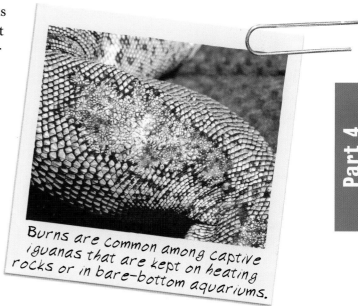

Burns are common among captive iguanas that are kept on heating rocks or in bare-bottom aquariums.

If the burn seems to be infected or if your iguana seems overly traumatized after being burned, seek veterinary attention.

Constipation

Iguanas normally defecate every day or every other day. If your iguana has not defecated for longer than that, he is constipated. Constipation can be caused by parasites, cool temperatures, change of diet, intestinal blockage, and infection. Sometimes you can remedy the problem, and sometimes you need the vet.

If your iguana is constipated, check your cage temperatures. If they are not in the recommended range, raise them. This could resolve the constipation.

To try to solve a constipation problem, soak your iguana in warm water. Rub his belly in the direction of his vent for several minutes. Then put him back in his enclosure. He should go within a day of this treatment. If not, you need to take him to the vet.

Diarrhea

Like constipation, diarrhea can have many causes, including a major change in the diet, parasites, infection, and stress. Diarrhea is not the same as runny stools. Runny stools occur once in a while, usually after feeding your iguana fruit. Diarrhea is watery feces combined with the iguana defecating frequently.

Rubberjaw

When talking about iguanas, you may hear mention of a disease called rubberjaw. Rubberjaw is a form of MBD, a deficiency of either calcium or vitamin D leading to improper deposition of calcium in the bones of the jaws. It is sometimes called this because in young iguanas the bones in the jaws are among of the first to show signs of the deficiency. They get soft and bent out of shape, deforming the iguana's face and—in severe cases—impeding its ability to eat. If you follow the lighting and feeding recommendations in this book, your iguana will never get rubberjaw.

Because diarrhea is so often caused by an infection and because your iguana can rapidly dehydrate, seek veterinary care as soon as you notice that your ig has diarrhea.

Metabolic Bone Disease

If you are feeding your ig a proper diet and he has an adequate source of ultraviolet light, your iguana will not get metabolic bone disease. However, you should be familiar with the signs just in case.

Iguanas that have MBD (also called fibrous osteodystrophy) have enlarged thighs, spinal abnormalities, soft or deformed jaws, trouble walking (due to fractures), twisted toes, and/or muscular tremors. The enlarged thighs and soft jaws generally occur earlier than the other signs. The two most often-noted signs of MBD are an inability to lift the body and tail tip above the surface when trying to move and exceptionally flexible upper and lower jaws.

If your iguana exhibits any of these signs, you need to get vet care. Additionally, you must review your husbandry to find out where you are going wrong. Check the diet you are feeding your iguana and the type of lighting you are offering. Start getting your iguana out into the sunlight.

Metabolic bone disease is very treatable if treatment is started early and husbandry issues are addressed promptly. Females that have had MBD may have problems successfully breeding in the future.

Mites

These are small arachnids that bite animals and feed on their blood. You can think of them as fleas for reptiles. The only positive side is that the mites that commonly infect reptiles cannot infect mammals. In addition, mites are not common on iguanas that are kept away from other reptiles. Generally, iguanas pick them up from other reptiles brought into the home.

Mites are hard to see, but you can detect them with some careful observation. You may see tiny dots moving around on your iguana. You may also see the silvery, dusty feces of the mites collected in the crevices of your ig's scales. I've found the best way to spot mites is to look in the water bowl–you'll see a number of tiny, round, blackish bugs drowned in the bottom of the bowl. If you see any of these signs, your ig has mites.

When you treat for mites, you have to destroy the ones not only on your ig but also in his enclosure. This can be difficult, given the size of the average iguana cage and how easily mites and their eggs can hide in tiny crevices.

The method I've had good results with is fairly nontoxic. I treat the affected lizard with some type of cooking oil by filling a basin with the oil and totally submerging the lizard in the oil. Because igs are so big, it may work better to liberally soak a cloth in oil and rub the entire body with it. Don't forget the armpits, bases of

Pest Strips and Mites

No-pest strips (dichlorvos) used to be the most recommended way of combating mites. However, for the past few years, more and more vets and keepers are urging people not to use them. The fumes that these products exude are toxic and have been implicated in the deaths of a number of iguanas and other reptiles. I strongly urge you not to use these for mite control.

Part 4

the spines, corners of the mouth, and eyelids. Afterward, dry off your perturbed iguana. Expect him to go into shed within the next few days.

While treating your ig, you need to eliminate the mites in the enclosure. Throw away anything in the cage that is disposable: substrate, disposable hide boxes, any climbing limbs that you aren't attached to. Don't just put them in the household garbage, or the mites will crawl out of the garbage and eventually get back to your iguana. Put them in a garbage bag, seal it up, and take it to the outside garbage cans.

To treat a small cage, I recommend a thorough disinfection with bleach. Soak all surfaces of the cage and furnishings and let the bleach sit on them for at least 15 minutes. Then rinse thoroughly. Because mite eggs are resistant to treatment, be prepared to repeat this procedure in about three to five weeks.

A new product called Provent-A-Mite seems to work wonders on controlling mites in the enclosure. You can spray all parts of the enclosure and put your ig into it right afterward without fear. Another mite-killing substance is ivermectin, available through your vet. Mix the ivermectin with water as directed and spray the enclosure with it. You can spray your iguana directly, but be careful to get none in his eyes or mouth.

Emergency!

If you notice any of the following, seek medical care for your iguana immediately:

Your iguana is not breathing

Your iguana has a large wound or a wound that will not stop bleeding

There is blood in your iguana's feces

A limb appears broken

Your iguana is paralyzed or not responding.

Mouth Rot

This infection of the gums and other oral tissues is as disgusting as it sounds. You will notice it as a thick, cheesy substance (pus) in your iguana's mouth. It will probably cause your iguana's breath to stink, and the surrounding tissues may look red and inflamed. The technical term for mouth rot is *stomatitis*. Other signs include loss of appetite (it becomes painful to eat), loss of teeth, and heavy salivation, especially if the saliva is thick or stringy.

Mouth rot requires veterinary treatment. The vet will culture the pus and prescribe an appropriate antibiotic. If you caught the infection in time, you won't have to worry about pureeing the food or

The Mummy Technique

If you have to restrain your iguana for medical care or to take a look at something yourself, you need to do so in a way that minimizes the chance that you and your ig will get hurt. If your scaly pet is socialized and well behaved, this may not be an issue. However, if you have one that is not, you will need a good restraining method.

I call this the Mummy Technique, because you are going to wrap up your belligerent ig in a towel, blanket, or some other material. Use something old, as it may get ripped or defecated on (or even bled on if you are unlucky). Something large is best. For Petey, I use an old comforter.

Assuming your iguana is as freaky as Petey, you will need to be fast. Throw the blanket or towel over the ig like a net; then tuck it under him as quickly and tightly as you can. Once you get that done, slowly and gently free your ig's head. Be careful that you do not get bitten. If you do not need access to his whole head, I recommend only exposing his snout. Many wild iguanas will become calm if their eyes are covered.

Once you have his snout free so he can breathe and he's firmly wrapped up, you have to slowly expose whatever area the vet needs to access or you need to check. During this procedure, speaking to your iguana in soft tones will also help keep him calm.

When you and/or the vet are done, take the mummy-wrapped and unhappy iguana back to his cage. Place him on the floor of the cage and unwrap him. Keep talking nicely to him. Be prepared to move quickly if he lunges at you.

I would never recommend using this technique on a friendly iguana, but I thought it was important to describe it for those of you that have your own version of Petey.

force-feeding your ig, but these are both real possibilities when dealing with mouth rot. Your vet will instruct on these procedures.

While your ig is being treated, keep his cage a little warmer than normal. Also, make sure you give him foods high in vitamin C. Mouth rot usually occurs only in herps that have a depressed immune system. Have your vet check your ig's immune function, and make sure you are keeping the enclosure warm enough and feeding a proper diet.

Prolapse

A prolapse is the protrusion of an organ or tissue through the vent. This is a very serious condition and requires veterinary care immediately. Common types of prolapses are cloacal, intestinal, and hemipenal, named for the organ or tissue that is protruding.

The causes of prolapse can be parasites, infection, egg-binding, or straining while constipated. Once the tissue is outside of the body, it will start to dry out and die. You must seek veterinary attention as soon as possible. While waiting to see the vet, keep the protruding organ damp and covered.

One method that herp keepers have found that sometimes resolves a prolapse is to soak the iguana in cool sugar-water. Dissolve a hefty amount of sugar in some water and soak your iguana. This can cause the tissue to disengorge, allowing your iguana to retract it. If this doesn't work within a few minutes, seek veterinary care.

Respiratory Infection

The signs of a respiratory infection are wheezing, lethargy, open-mouthed breathing, and discharge from the mouth or nose (not the normal salt elimination). In advanced cases, the iguana will make bubbling noises while breathing and stop eating.

Infections of the respiratory system are almost always caused by the temperature being too cool or by the iguana's enclosure having too little humidity. You must make sure the temperature and humidity are adequate. When your iguana has a respiratory infection, raise the temperature of the enclosure by five degrees or so. The higher temperature will give your iguana's immune system a boost. If the infection does not clear up in a day or two after raising the temperature, get your iguana to the vet.

Wounds

No matter the cause, any open wound your iguana suffers requires your attention. For the most part, you can treat them like you would a wound on yourself. Clean out the area with cool water and a mild soap. Pat dry. Apply an antibiotic ointment. If the wound is not bleeding much, leave it unbandaged. If you have to bandage it, use sterile dressing and medical tape, not commercial adhesive strips. Adhesive strips will come off too easily and subsequently might be ingested by your iguana. Keep an eye on the wound for signs of infection. If it looks infected, your ig needs to see the vet.

If the wound is very deep, doesn't stop bleeding, or has a protruding bone, your iguana needs immediate medical attention.

Making More Iguanas

A Guide to Iguana Reproduction

Although it is wisest to own only one iguana, many people—myself included—end up with more than one. Those of us who end up with a pair often consider breeding them. Others who really love their iguanas think it would be a great experience to get their ig a mate and have baby iguanas. This chapter will help you to not only successfully breed your iguanas but also to decide whether or not you should do so. Even if you have no intentions of breeding your ig, this chapter has some valuable information for you, so don't skip it.

Hard to Breed?

Despite the abundance of iguanas in captivity and

Adult male iguanas usually exhibit some orange coloration on their legs and feet.

How Old Do They Need to Be?

Sexual maturity in iguanas is actually more related to size than age. Generally, females are able to breed when they are around 10 inches long, snout to vent. Males can breed at 6 inches SVL. Usually, iguanas will reach this length when they are two to three years old. Variations in care will cause differences in the onset of sexual maturity.

I do not recommend breeding females at the minimum size or age. Breeding puts a lot of stress on the body of a female iguana. At two to three years of age, she is still growing pretty rapidly, and her body is filling out. Breeding her then may stunt her or cause other problems further on down the road.

My advice is to wait until your female is at least three to four years old and 12 inches or more snout to vent. This will increase your chances of both having healthy baby iguanas and a healthy, long-lived mom iguana.

the fact that the standard of iguana care continues to rise as the years go on, breeding iguanas is still a relatively rare event. As a whole, iguanas do not seem to breed well in captivity.

There are many reasons for this. Mostly, iguanas do not breed easily because, typically, they are given inadequate space and inadequate diets. Further, they often do not get enough ultraviolet light. Iguanas need to be kept in excellent conditions if they are to breed, and, sadly, most iguana owners do not provide such conditions. Very few iguanas in captivity have sufficient space to live in from day to day, let alone breed in.

One reason that really stands out to me is that there is a lack of information on breeding iguanas available to the average reptile keeper. This is caused by a general lack of interest by the mainstream herp community in breeding iguanas. Iguanas are inexpensive and are viewed as a sort of "beginner's lizard" by experienced herpers. Therefore, few herpers view breeding iguanas as something interesting or valuable to undertake or write about.

Lastly, iguanas can be picky when it comes to breeding. Pairs may not like one another, the lighting may not be perfect, the female may dislike the nestbox, and many other small things that bother the iguanas can inhibit breeding.

For these reasons and probably many others that humans are not yet aware of, successfully breeding iguanas is challenging. Success has become more frequent, but it is still noteworthy.

Harsh Realities

Before you go ahead and attempt to breed your iguanas, sit down and ask yourself why you want to breed iguanas. Your answer to this question is important, as it will in large part determine what you get out of the experience.

Profit

There are few common reasons why people breed iguanas. Unfortunately, one of the most common is money. These keepers think that they can get their iguanas to breed, hatch out the eggs, and sell the young to pet stores or through the local paper for profit. These keepers are mistaken.

The reality of the trade in green iguanas is that they are very inexpensive to buy. If you bought your iguanas at a pet store, you can be sure the pet store bought those iguanas from a wholesaler for probably less than half of your cost. Furthermore, if you knew what the wholesalers paid the importers, you would probably cringe. Therefore, in most cases, it will cost you more to produce those iguanas than what pet stores or buyers will be willing to pay, especially if you want to raise the young for a bit to put some good growth on them, rather than selling them right from the egg.

Because pet stores can buy their iguanas so cheaply, they will probably not be willing to buy yours. You can try to explain that your captive-bred iguanas are healthier and already adapted to captivity—and you will almost certainly be correct—but because customers buy the imported ones without a second thought, the pet store isn't likely to really care. I'm sure there are pet stores that would much rather buy captive-bred iguanas from local breeders than buy imported ones from wholesalers, but those stores are few and far between.

Juvenile green iguanas are often bright green and very hard to resist.

Part 4

Oops! MY Iguanas Mated

It is possible that your iguanas will mate without you actually intending them to mate. This presents no problems if you don't mind, but if you don't want to breed your iguanas, you have some issues to deal with.

If your iguanas mate and you don't want to deal with all the babies, you still have to provide for the female's health and well-being through the gravid period. You'll still have to provide her with a nest box to prevent egg-binding. However, once the eggs are laid, just don't incubate them. If you don't incubate them, they won't hatch. That solves your problem with having a score or more of unwanted baby iguanas.

This may sound cruel or heartless to you. If so, consider whether it is more cruel to destroy unwanted eggs or to have them hatch into unwanted babies that may get inadequate care, end up in animal shelters, or die of illness or neglect.

You might be able to sell healthy, captive-bred iguanas at a reptile expo. However, selling at a show is not without costs. There will be the cost of the table, which ranges widely in price depending on the expo. Then there are the costs of your transportation, food, lodging (if needed), and permits. Most states do require some form of permit to sell animals within their borders, and the permits usually have an annual fee. Lastly, you will need a tax identification number and have to charge sales tax at the expo. If you are only selling iguanas, these expenses will hardly be worth the bother, if they are worth it at all.

Remember that you are likely to have 20 to 40 baby iguanas to sell. It will take you a long time to sell that many through your local paper or to the pet stores in your state. While you are waiting to sell all the babies, you will have to be feeding them, lighting them, heating them, and vetting them if necessary. All of these things cost money, cutting into your profit.

If you want to breed your iguanas to make money, think again.

The Experience

Another reason for breeding your iguanas is just to have the experience of breeding them. This is not a bad motivation, because it is fascinating, educational, and exciting to breed iguanas (or any other herps, for that matter).

There are a couple of issues that crop up with this motivation. One is that there are some inherent risks for the parent iguanas in the breeding process. Granted, most iguanas live through breeding just fine, but do you want to risk your beloved pet just to have the experience of breeding iguanas? Only you can decide that.

Part 4

The other issue with this motivation–and with all motivations for breeding iguanas, actually–is what to do with the babies. If you can't sell them or find homes for them, are you prepared to keep them? If the answer is "no," then it is not ethical to breed them.

It's Natural

If you think that it's just natural for your iguanas to breed and that you are somehow depriving them if you don't let them breed, consider the many ways in which your iguana already lives a less than natural life. He is heated by lights, not the sun. He eats food from a produce department, not pulled off the branches of trees. He is not subjected to predation, parasites, harsh weather, drought, or any of the other hazards of a natural iguana life.

It is certainly natural for iguanas to breed. It is also natural that many of the eggs will not survive to hatch. In nature, the hatchlings disperse far from each other soon after leaving the nest. Most of those hatchlings will not survive to adulthood, falling victim to predation, illness, accident, and bad genetics before ever having their own offspring. In nature, no one has to worry about what to do with all the baby iguanas.

If I still haven't dissuaded you from breeding your iguanas, then hold on. It's going to be a bumpy ride.

Is It a He or a She?

If you want to breed any type of animal, one of the first things you need to know is how to tell the males from the females. Without at least one of each, you won't get very far.

The differences between male and female iguanas are covered in the chapter on iguana biology. For convenience, I've included a short checklist of the differences below. For this checklist, I am assuming that the iguanas in question are adults. It is very difficult to sex babies and juveniles.

Females are not as brightly colored as males, but they are usually calmer and often make better pets.

1. Males have large and rather blocky heads;

The femoral pores of male green iguanas are larger and more pronounced than in females.

female heads are smaller and more slender.

2. Males have a much larger dewlap than females (in some populations of iguanas the difference is not very obvious).

3. Males have larger nuchal and dorsal crests.

4. Males reach a greater overall size; females rarely grow to more than 5 feet in length.

5. Males develop enlarged jowls.

6. Males have hemipenal bulges at the base of the tail.

7. The femoral pores of the male are larger and secrete a waxy substance; a female's femoral pores are small and do not secrete anything.

8. During breeding season, the forequarters of most males will become orangish.

9. By looking at all of these characteristics, you should be able to tell male iguanas from female iguanas, at least when looking at adults.

Another way of sexing iguanas is to probe them. This involves inserting a tool specifically made for this purpose into the vent of an iguana and noting how deep inside it will go. You should have an experienced person show you how to do this, as there is the potential to cause your iguana harm.

One high-tech way to sex iguanas is to have their DNA analyzed. There are companies that specialize in sexing animals (primarily birds, but also reptiles) by looking at their chromosomes. At least one of these companies advertises in herp publications. Your vet may know of others or even offer the service at his or her office.

The procedure involves going to your vet and having him or her draw a blood sample from

Part 4

your iguana. The blood is sent to the company, and technicians there examine it. They are looking for sex chromosomes in the blood cells. (For those of you who are biologically minded, iguanas and other reptiles–and birds–have nucleated blood cells, so there are plenty of chromosomes in their blood cells. The red blood cells of mammals lose their chromosomes during development.) Once they make the determination, they send the results to you or your vet. Of course, this is not free, but I have heard the price is reasonable. This is definitely the most accurate way of sexing your iguanas short of seeing them mate or seeing one lay eggs.

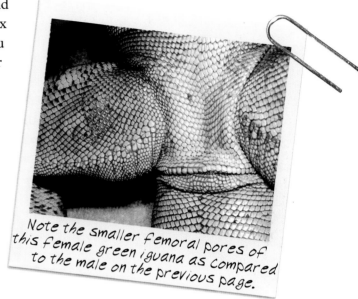

Note the smaller femoral pores of this female green iguana as compared to the male on the previous page.

Setting the Mood

Breeding iguanas is not like breeding rabbits; you can't just put them together and let nature take its course. While that approach may work, you will have much more success if you provide your iguanas with seasonal variations approximating the change of seasons they would experience in nature.

Pre-breeding Care

If your iguanas are getting sub-optimal care, there is little chance they will successfully breed. In the years leading up to their adulthood and sexual maturity, their care must be top-notch. The better the iguanas' care, the more likely they are to breed. If they are not in perfect health, the chances of them successfully reproducing will be lessened. It is wise to have your iguanas checked by a vet before starting the breeding process.

A critical component is the diet. Their diet must be perfect. It is especially important that the female's diet be the best it can be. She will be the one who has to produce the embryos and eggs. Her nutrition greatly affects the number of eggs she lays, how likely the egg are to hatch, and how likely the babies are to survive. If she is not getting enough calcium, her body will take it from her bones to make the eggshells; this could leave her in a very bad condition. Make sure that your parents-to-be have an excellent diet.

Along with the diet, all other care parameters should be excellent. This includes heating, ultraviolet light, humidity, and adequate space for each adult.

Part 4

Among herpers, this is called *cycling* your animals. However, it should be noted that iguanas are one of the relatively few reptiles that often mate without any cycling. Cycling them helps ensure that they not only mate, but also that they are fertile and have viable offspring.

The reason you want to cycle your igs is that, in their natural habitat, iguanas breed only during a certain period of the year. They have a breeding season, much like other wild animals. By changing the temperature, humidity, and/or photoperiod, you are creating seasonal changes in the captive environment.

Of course, you cannot create changes that precisely mimic the natural variations. What you are doing is tricking your igs' bodies into thinking that the breeding season is coming. If their brains and gonads think the breeding season is coming, they will produce the hormones that trigger reproductive behavior and fertility.

Creating changes of seasons in your iguanas' enclosure may sound like a daunting task, but it is actually easier than you would think. The key here is that you don't have to *precisely* mimic the natural seasonal changes. Often you just need to create some variation in the conditions, generally being a nice, ideal season and a less nice, sub-par season. Don't be alarmed: I am not suggesting you keep your iguanas in bad captive environments. I'm just saying that you need to approximate what happens in nature. It will not harm your iguanas, although there is some stress associated with breeding. The vast majority of iguanas will come through breeding just fine.

There are several environmental factors you can manipulate in order to convince your iguanas to breed. The most obvious are photoperiod, temperature, and humidity. Photoperiod appears to be the most important parameter, and usually you will only need to change the photoperiod and possibly the temperature. We'll include the humidity in the discussion, just in case your iguanas are more stubborn than most.

Photoperiod

I'm sure that you are aware that the length of daylight changes over the course of the year. There are more hours of daylight in the summer and fewer in winter. Many animals and plants use the changes in daylight as ways of timing their growth and reproduction. Green iguanas are one of the animals that use lighting cues to regulate their breeding cycle.

You probably have already realized controlling the photoperiod to breed your iguanas means you are going to have the lights on for fewer hours in the "winter" and have them on for more hours in the "summer." However, you can't just make the changes overnight. It doesn't go from winter to summer in a day, so neither should you make such drastic changes in your iguanas' photoperiods. The changes should be gradual.

Most keepers use a 12-hour light and 12-hour dark (12:12) cycle for their iguanas. This is fine for everyday keeping, but you will be changing the light-dark ratio for breeding. During the winter, you should use a 10:14 light/dark cycle. In the summer, reverse them, so you have a 14:10 light/dark cycle. You might be able to get away with less variation; it will depend on your iguanas.

Green iguanas need a photoperiod of no less than 8 hours of daylight and 16 hours of darkness.

You should make the changes in no more than one hour increments, spread out over some time. For example, starting with your normal 12:12 cycle and moving toward the winter, you might cut the amount of light by 15 minutes one week, 15 more the next, and so on. In a month you will have cut an hour of daylight out of the photoperiod. Continue this until you reach the day length you desire.

You could make larger changes, but I would recommend changing the photoperiod no more than a half-hour at one time. You should also let your igs adjust to that change for at least a week before changing the photoperiod any more. If you do less gradual changes, you could throw your iguanas' hormonal rhythms out of whack. This could delay breeding or even cause your pair to skip breeding for that year.

Once you have the day length at the desired 10 hours, maintain your iguanas on this photoperiod for several weeks. Then, in the same gradual fashion, lengthen the time the lights stay on until you reach 14 hours of light and 10 hours of dark.

Iguanas require a warm and humid enclosure.

It will be far easier to cycle your iguanas if the enclosure lights are on timers. This way you just have to change the settings on the timers, rather than remember at what times each day you need to turn on and turn off the lights for that particular week or month.

Temperature

Another factor that might affect breeding is temperature. The seasonal change in temperatures is just one more thing that iguanas may cue in on for the timing of their breeding.

Changes in temperature over the course of the year will be relatively small. Iguanas have a narrow range at which they will continue to be healthy and happy. You do not want your temperatures to go beyond the healthy/happy range.

During your artificial winter, decrease the temperature of your iguana's basking spot to 88° to 90°F. The rest of the iguana's cage can stay the normal temperature. At night, you can safely allow temperatures to drop to 68° to 70°F.

The normal keeping temperatures recommended in the housing chapter serve as the summer temperatures. You do not need to change the temperatures as gradually as you do the photoperiod because the differences are so small.

Note that in changing the photoperiod–assuming you are heating your iguanas with lights–you will be changing the temperature.

Humidity

Although seasonal changes in humidity occur in the iguana's natural habitat, humidity does not seem to play an important role in the timing of breeding, at least in captivity. Because humidity follows a seasonal cycle similar to day length and temperature, perhaps iguanas did not need to evolve to follow all three factors.

If you have already created seasonal variations in photoperiod and temperature and your iguanas have still not successfully bred, you can try adding variation in humidity to the

Part 4

equation. As you reduce the hours of daylength, you will reduce the humidity. At the peak of your manmade winter, the humidity should be roughly 60 to 70 percent. Gradually raise the humidity (through more spraying, a larger bowl of water, or however you need to raise it) to between 85 and 90 percent. It may help to give your iguanas frequent showers and soaks during this period, as well.

To manipulate the humidity so finely, you will certainly need an accurate humidity gauge (hygrometer). Good digital ones are available at better electronics stores.

It Didn't Work

Okay, you cycled the photoperiod, the temperature, and even the humidity. Your iguanas did not breed. What went wrong?

The problem is a lot of things might've gone wrong. Below is a list of possible problems and some solutions. Any of these can hinder breeding, but to be sure what the problem is, you will have to think about and observe your iguanas carefully. Consultation with a veterinarian is likely to be helpful.

You have two iguanas of the same sex. Double-check your sexing.

Your iguanas are too young or too small. Give them another year of growth and try again.

Not enough space. Cramped iguanas often will not breed. Build or buy a larger enclosure.

Not enough ultraviolet light. Add another UV light or–even better–get your iguanas out in the natural sunlight. Simply exposing iguanas to unfiltered sunlight on a regular basis often does the trick. Petey and Kermit did not breed until I moved. In my new apartment, an open window provided them with unfiltered sunlight. They started breeding the following autumn.

You are not feeding them enough. If they are not getting enough energy and nutrients, sex will not be a priority for their bodies.

They have parasites or some other ailment. If their bodies are using energy to fight off disease, your iguanas may not have the energy to breed. Consult a veterinarian.

Part 4

They just don't feel that way about one another. Sometimes a given pair of iguanas will just refuse to breed with one another. Try keeping them out of one another's sight and scent for a few months. If that doesn't work, network to find an iguana or two for a breeding loan.

Breeding Behavior

Iguanas go through a number of behavioral changes when they come into season. Unfortunately, most of these changes are not pleasant ones for their human friends.

Males

Back in the section on anatomy, I mentioned that male iguanas in breeding season seem to think of nothing besides breeding. When you reach this stage of your iguana's life, you'll get to experience it firsthand.

A Probing Question

One way to sex iguanas is to probe them, which involves the use of special tools called sexing probes. These can be purchased at herp shows or through Internet herp suppliers, but few pet stores carry them.

The sexing probes are basically slender rods of stainless steel with a tiny ball on the end. They are inserted into the cloaca of a reptile to determine its sex. The tiny ball helps prevent the probe from causing an injury. Not all reptiles can be probed successfully.

Probing is a delicate procedure, and you should definitely have someone experienced show you how to do it. Performed incorrectly, probing can injure the iguana, possibly causing infertility, infection, and internal bleeding.

To probe an iguana, you select the proper-sized probe and lubricate it with sterile lubricating jelly. Then, gently insert the probe into the vent in the direction of the tail. Usually, you will have to move the probe toward the body first and then move toward the tail. Push gently off to the side until you feel resistance.

The depth the probe penetrates tells you the sex of the iguana. If it is a male, the probe will slide into the hemipene and penetrate rather deeply. If the iguana is a female, there will be no hemipene to enter, so the probe will not penetrate deeply at all.

Again, this procedure must be done delicately. Do not try it until someone shows you how. I've included this description for the sake of completeness, not to give instructions to the inexperienced.

Male iguanas go through many behavioral changes during breeding season. Depending on the individual, these may be mild changes or your iguana may act as though demonically possessed. In my experience, males that are owned by women or that are housed near female iguanas go through the most drastic changes.

The most common behavioral changes seen in the sexed-males are restlessness, loss of appetite, and frequent head-bobbing. As the male becomes more concerned with breeding, he'll care less about food. Because of this fact, you must provide an excellent diet during the rest of the year. Keep offering food throughout the breeding season. He will eat a little on occasion, so make sure there is food available.

Sometimes male iguanas become strangely attentive to women owners or female members of the household during breeding season. The iguana will follow them around, seek out attention, and trying to maintain long periods of physical contact. This can progress to attempting to mount and mate with human women.

Male iguanas in season have been known to attempt mating with a number of non-iguana objects and organisms. They may mount your furniture, banisters, a climbing log, your arm, a particular piece of your clothing, or other household pets. They seem to be most attracted to green or blue objects.

Without wishing to be indelicate, I should mention that male iguanas also masturbate. They will evert one or both hemipenes and rub them on an object (or person!) until they ejaculate. This does not harm the iguana and is quite natural. Such behavior, however, can stain or ruin furniture and clothing.

One of the most frequently discussed behavioral changes of males is aggression. Sexed-up males can be downright nasty. Don't think that just because you have a puppy-dog friendly ig he won't become a terror in November. Once those super-size testes start pumping out the hormones, you might think your iguana has been possessed. Like other reproductive behaviors, the extent to which aggressiveness develops depends on the individual and other factors.

Large, aggressive male iguanas can be dangerous animals. If your iguana becomes aggressive during the breeding season, you must be very cautious. This is especially true of

Part 4

female owners, who seem to attract more of the aggressive iguana's belligerence than male owners.

There are ways of protecting yourself from an aggressive ig. First, assert your dominance. Don't cower or run from the enclosure. Second, do not wear any colors that seem to escalate his aggression. Green and blue are the most common trigger colors. Wear thick clothing that will make any bites or whips less painful and less damaging. You could also wear leather gloves. Watch your back, and keep your face out of tail range.

If your iguana gets too aggressive for you to handle, you can try some things that might calm him down. Shut off the ultraviolet light for a few days and eliminate any exposure to natural sunlight. If this doesn't work, move him to a dark room for a day or two. Make sure the room is warm enough, but it should be completely dark.

You can also try to give him something to take his aggression out on. This could be a stuffed animal, an old shirt, an old sneaker, or anything that attracts his attention that is not harmful to your iguana. Something green or blue and that smells like you will probably be the best.

If you have two males, you should never let them near one another during breeding season. Male iguanas in breeding condition normally fight, sometimes producing pretty nasty wounds. In captivity, the loser of such a fight has nowhere to get away from the winner, so the winner often keeps thrashing the loser. The result is usually a dead or severely wounded iguana. *Keep males separated during the breeding season.*

If you have two males and you handle one, wash your hands before handling the other. If you smell like the other male, you are more likely to be attacked.

Remember that the breeding season and the associated changes in your iguana are temporary. In a few months, you'll have your sweet ole ig back.

Females
Female iguanas do not go through nearly the drastic changes that the males do, but there are some changes you should be aware of.

Mostly, females in breeding season are just crankier than normal. They may not want to be touched and may hiss or display at you more often. Very occasionally, female iguanas actually get nicer than normal during the breeding season.

Like males, females may go off their food and become restless when in breeding condition. This is especially true if your female is gravid.

Mating

Once your iguanas are behaving like they are ready to breed, you can introduce them to one another. Most iguana keepers believe it works out best if you bring the female into the male's enclosure. Males feel most secure on their own turf. If you bring the male to the female, he might be more worried that the male he assumes is controlling this territory is going to come and fight for it than he is about mating. Therefore, take the female to the male.

Iguana Went-A-Courting

Mating begins with a courtship display by the male. He approaches the female while making very rapid head-bobbing motions. The male frequently approaches from behind. The female may arch her tail. That's pretty much all the courtship.

However, courtship may occur dozens of times for several days or weeks before actual mating occurs. You can't just arrange to put the male and female together for an afternoon and be done with the mating process. You will have to keep introducing the female to the male over the course of the breeding season.

Unless you have a gigantic cage with plenty of hiding areas, do not leave them together, as the male could get aggressive. My iguanas are now separated primarily because Petey became overly aggressive during their third breeding season together. Owners have found their females killed by their males when the pair was left unattended. Don't let this happen to your igs.

The Nitty-Gritty

After a few bouts of courting, your iguanas will finally complete the act. The male will come up behind the female or even climb over her. He will firmly grasp her nape with his mouth.

Part 4

Together or Separate?

You may be wondering if you should keep your male and female together or separated prior to breeding. I think iguanas fare best when housed singly. Also, when male and female iguanas are kept together, they sometimes show no interest in breeding with one another. Once separated and reintroduced, pairs that formerly were indifferent to each other often become very amorous.

Keep your male and female separated until they are ready to breed. Then, introduce your female into the male's enclosure. If your male is like most iguanas in breeding season, he will bob his head at your female a few times, then proceed quickly to biting her neck and mounting.

At this point, if the female is receptive, she will lift her tail, allowing the male access to her vent. If she is not receptive, she will thrash about and try to get away. The male will usually pursue an unreceptive female and attempt mating again. This can go on for days, until the female ig becomes sexually receptive.

Once the male has mounted and the female has consented to the mating, the male moves his vent next to hers. One or both of his hemipenes will evert and become erect. He'll insert one into the female's vent.

Iguanas may stay "locked-up" (the term herpers use for two reptiles that are copulating) for 10 to 30 minutes. During this time, you may see the abdomen of the male contracting. Assumedly, these contractions are pushing semen along the male reproductive tract and into the vent of the female. The female usually remains quite still, but she may walk around a bit, dragging the attached male with her. Once copulation is over, the iguanas separate and do their own thing.

Iguanas usually mate more than once per breeding season. In fact, they may mate several times a day for a week or two. After this time, the pair may lose interest in one another, or the female will stop being receptive. You can now stop introducing them and prepare for the eggs.

Mating in iguanas can be very rough, and it is quite common for a female to end up with nasty lacerations on her neck. These normally heal up without complications, although the wounds may leave scars. It is wise to keep the mating wounds clean with hydrogen peroxide or povidone-iodine.

The Mother-To-Be

Gravid females need some special care if you expect them to develop and lay viable eggs. If you have been providing excellent housing conditions and a balanced diet to your female ig all along, you have already done much to ensure her and her babies' health.

Signs of Egg-binding

Egg-binding (also called dystocia) is a serious condition of gravid female iguanas. Basically, it is the inability to lay eggs that are ready to be laid.

This can be caused by a number of factors. Most frequently the cause is either not having an appropriate nesting site or having a prior history of metabolic bone disease. There are a number of other causes, including the female being too young for breeding. Egg-bound females need immediate vet attention if they are to survive. If this condition persists for too long, parts of the oviduct can die and rot, causing severe and often fatal illness.

You should suspect your female is egg-bound if it is over eight weeks since she bred and you observe any of the following:

Continued digging, as if trying to dig a nest, especially if other symptoms are present or it is over nine weeks since breeding

Lethargy or depression

Straining as if she is unable to pass something

Grayish coloration

Sunken eyes

Lack of interest in food and water.

If you suspect egg-binding, seek veterinary care immediately.

One thing that you should do with a gravid female is to adjust the temperature of the hot spot to the upper end of the suggested range (100°F). Gravid females often like to stay slightly warmer than normal. Prevent any exposure to temperatures below 75°F during her gravidity.

Gravid females tend to be very inactive. They will spend most of their time basking and doing little else. They may be moody and not want to be touched. This is especially true in the late stages of gestation. Respect her wishes in this. It's also possible that she may want to be petted and cuddled more than normal.

Feed your female as much as she will eat. Include more of the high-calcium vegetables than you might normally. You should also supplement the calcium in the diet twice a week or so. She will be using a lot of calcium to make eggshells.

You want to encourage her to eat early on, because as gestation progresses, she'll probably stop eating. She will continue drinking and may even drink a lot more than she did before she was gravid. The appetite generally starts to slack around a month after breeding. Around six weeks after mating, the female's appetite becomes very depressed. She may eat only a mouthful each day or may skip a day or two between meals. Some females stop eating entirely.

I recommend you take your ig in to see the vet as soon as you suspect she's gravid. The vet can assess her overall health to see how likely it is that she'll be successful at developing and laying eggs. You'll also want to discuss with your vet how to get in touch with him or her if an emergency arises during gestation.

It is especially important to take your female to see the vet if she has had metabolic bone disease in the past. The MBD might have distorted her pelvis, making it difficult or impossible to lay the eggs. An ultrasound or radiograph should reveal this. If so, you'll need to discuss surgically removing the eggs with your vet.

Near the end of gestation, the female will become very restless. She'll start prowling the bottom of her cage endlessly. She may start to dig in the corners or the litter pan. If you haven't given her a nesting box at this point, do so immediately. She's ready to lay her eggs.

A female iguana generally lays her eggs around eight weeks after mating. By this time, her abdomen will be greatly distended. When it gets near her laying time, you will be able to see the outlines of individual eggs.

One of the reasons the appetite of a gravid iguana drops so much is that the eggs fill most of the space of her abdomen, leaving almost no room for food. A female iguana can lay anywhere from 12 to 60 eggs. Older and larger iguanas lay the biggest clutches. Each one will be around an inch and a half in length and weigh less than an ounce. The clutch as a whole may weigh a third of the female's total weight.

The Nest Box

Iguanas will not normally lay their eggs just anywhere. They need to build a nest. In captivity, you have to provide them with that nest or the materials they need in order to build it themselves.

In nature, iguanas nest in sunny areas of sandy soil, often a beach or riverbank. They find a spot they like and begin to dig. They will dig a tunnel that can be from 2 to 4 feet in length, the end 2 to 3 feet underground. The female lays her eggs at the end of the tunnel and fills it in afterward. When she's done, it will be difficult to tell that she dug a nest at all.

If you are keeping your iguana outside, you can provide a nesting area by digging into the soil and mixing it with sand. Other keepers put a deep sandbox in the enclosure and make the sand slightly moist. This provides a nice, semi-natural egg-laying site. The only problem for the keeper is finding the eggs after she lays them.

Indoors, the situation is much different. You will have to build a nest box for your ig. What you make the box out of is not critically important. What is important is that it be a place that your female recognizes as a decent place to lay her eggs. A good nest box has the following qualities: the inside is large and roomy, there is a tunnel to get in and out of it, it's dark inside, and there is a suitable nesting medium inside. Additionally, the box should allow you easy access, so you can check for the eggs without causing a disruption to it.

You will have to make a nest box that fits these requirements, as no one has yet marketed an iguana nest box. Some possible choices for the nest box include a large, covered kitty-litter box, a large garbage can, a plastic storage bin (cut a hole in the lid), or a dog house. You can also build a nesting box out of wood, melamine, or a similar material. A large PVC pipe can provide a tunnel into the nest box, but make sure it is big enough for the female to get in and out of easily.

The nest box should be simple and easy-to-clean.

When Kermit was gravid, I used a kitchen garbage can. I taped the lid on and cut a hole in the side. This worked out pretty well. If I were to do it again, I'd use a larger garbage can.

There are a couple of different materials you can use for a nesting medium. Keepers have had success using sand, sterile organic potting soil, a mix of

When Do They Breed?

Iguanas typically go through their breeding season from October to February or March. There is much variation among individuals, and this will also depend on exactly how you are cycling yours.

If you are cycling your iguanas, they will breed at the peak of your winter—the shortest daylengths and lowest temperatures.

sand and soil, and vermiculite. Whichever you choose, you have to moisten it for your female to find it acceptable. You don't want it too moist; if it is soggy, your female will not be able to dig in it. The consistency you want is for it to be just damp enough to build a tunnel without the walls collapsing. The nesting medium should be deep. Fill your nest box up so that there is just room enough for the female to fit inside.

The top of the nest box should be warmed. Additionally, a light might attract your female to the spot. Do not warm the bottom of the nest box. In nature, soil gets cooler as you dig down. Heat coming up from the bottom of the nest box may result in cooked eggs.

The nest box should be placed in the enclosure at least two weeks before you expect her to lay her eggs. If your iguana roams free, put the box in a warm, sunny spot near her usual hangouts. Having the box available for so long before egg-laying allows your female to get used to the box. If you put it in the enclosure right when you expect eggs, she may be scared of the new thing in her habitat and avoid it. Allow her unrestricted access to the nest box.

Your female will probably go in and out of the box several times before actually laying her eggs. She may even dig some test holes in it. Be prepared for a mess, as iguanas normally flip a lot of the nesting medium out of the box. Monitor how much substrate remains in the box, so you can add more if it gets low.

You must check the box every day for eggs. The sooner you move them from the nest box to the incubator, the better their chance for survival. Also, if you don't check every day and the eggs go bad, they could draw flies and other vermin. Check the box when the female is not inside it. If she's inside when you open it, you could spook her, causing her to abandon the box as a nest site. It's also possible she'll lay her eggs elsewhere even if you provide a box.

You should be able to tell when your iguana lays her eggs just by looking at her. Once her eggs are laid, she'll look terrible. Her abdomen will be a flabby bag of nothing. It'll just look empty. The difference between just before laying and just afterward is dramatic.

Post-Natal Care

After the female lays her eggs, she'll be in rough shape. Remember that she hasn't eaten well in at least two weeks and that she spent a lot of her metabolic resources on making eggs.

As soon as possible after the laying, give your female a long soak. She will be dehydrated, and a soaking will allow her to replenish some of her fluids. Check her frequently during the bath. She will be weak and tired; if you aren't observing her she could pass out and drown.

Once she has been soaked and is back in her cage, offer her some food with some calcium supplement. A little fruit may be a good idea, as this will provide a quick boost to her blood sugar and some much-needed calories. She may not eat much, but she will most likely take a few mouthfuls.

In the next few weeks, feed her as much as she will eat. For the first few days after laying, she may not eat much at one time, as her stomach will still be small. I recommend keeping food available at all times. Add a vitamin/mineral and calcium supplement to her food for the first week after laying. After this, supplement her food weekly. If she is thin, you can add some high-fat items to her food, like avocado (without the skin), soybeans, a few drops of some vegetable oil, or shredded coconut. Don't overdo it with these items, but adding them to a couple of meals for a week or two will cause no harm.

Within two or three months, your mommy ig should have regained the weight she lost during gravidity. Her tail and hips should be nice and round again, and her eyes should no longer have that sunken look. Her color should have returned to normal by this time. If she still looks underweight or otherwise "off" or if her behavior has not returned to normal, seek help from a veterinarian.

Incubating the Eggs

In nature, female iguanas lay their eggs in areas that are likely to provide them with the conditions they need to hatch successfully. Even mother iguanas in the wild get it wrong sometimes, and clutches fail to hatch. In captivity, it is up to the iguana's owners to provide the eggs with the necessary conditions.

Part 4

This incubator is large enough to incubate three different clutches of eggs at the same time.

Iguana eggs are adapted to incubate underground in tropical conditions. They will not incubate successfully if just left in the nest box or put in a box in a cabinet. You need to provide them with adequate temperature and humidity. If you live in a tropical or subtropical climate, you may just need to provide the proper humidity and leave them in the garage or garden shed.

Iguana eggs hatch best when kept at 85° to 87°F. They need to be kept humid but not soaking wet. The relative humidity in the air of an incubator should be around 90 percent.

The easiest way to provide iguana eggs with proper conditions is to use an incubator. You can buy one from a number of sources including herp expos, online pet suppliers, and feed stores. Make sure the one you buy will hold the correct temperature and humidity.

It is less expensive to make an incubator, but homemade incubators often do not hold the temperature and humidity as accurately as a purchased one. However, using the incubator I made, I've hatched out bearded dragons, kingsnakes, corn snakes, chameleons, banded geckos, savannah monitors, and other species of reptiles. Sadly, I did not hatch out iguanas. I think the eggs dried out too much before I got them to the incubator.

There are a number of ways to make an incubator. I'm going to share how I made mine. Other designs are not necessarily wrong. If they can maintain adequate temperatures and humidity, they will probably work fine.

My incubator is made out of a Styrofoam shipping box with an intact lid (used for shipping fish; pet stores will often give these away), a 25-watt submersible fish tank heater, a thermometer, two bricks, and some water. Put the bricks in the bottom of the shipping box. Fill with water to the top of the bricks. Put the heater in the water and plug it in. The thermometer has to be situated inside the incubator so that it is measuring the temperature of the air, not the water. I found this easiest to do with a digital thermometer that had a remote probe. I simply ran the probe through a small notch carved in the rim (the same notch the cord for the heater runs out) and let it dangle there. The bricks will serve as platforms to put the egg boxes on once you have eggs.

Set up the incubator at least a week before you have eggs. You'll need to fiddle with the settings on the heater to get the temperature right. The heat generated evaporates the water and keeps the air inside the incubator at a sufficient relative humidity. You will need to add some water periodically. I suggest using distilled water, as it has no chlorine or other additives.

When your iguana lays her eggs, transfer them to an egg box. The most common egg box is a plastic food storage container with holes poked in it. For a while I used the plastic jugs that my kitty litter came in. I cut them down to a depth of about 6 inches for lizards other than iguanas. Some baby lizards were able to get out of these and I would find them swimming in the incubator water.

You need an incubation medium to put the eggs on inside the egg box. All of the following media have been used successfully: sand, vermiculite, paper towels, perlite, and foam rubber. I've found vermiculite to be the most common and probably the best.

Add enough medium to the egg box to create a depth of nearly double the diameter of the egg. For iguanas, this is about 2 inches. Add some water to create a consistency similar to that of the nesting box. The substrate should be moist, but not soggy.

Bad Eggs

A good rule of thumb when breeding iguanas or any other reptiles is that if you aren't absolutely certain an egg is bad, treat it as if it were good. Sometimes eggs that you suspect are bad hatch into healthy offspring.

You can be sure an egg is bad if it does any of the following: stinks, collapses, grows mold or fungus, or has maggots in it. Short of any of these things happening, I always leave eggs in the incubator, because you never can be certain if they will hatch or not.

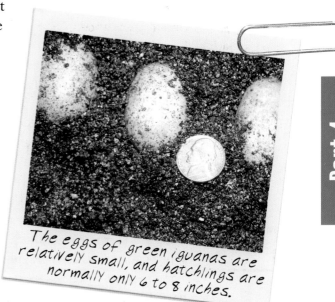

The eggs of green iguanas are relatively small, and hatchlings are normally only 6 to 8 inches.

Part 4

Once you have the medium ready, carefully place the eggs in it. Push them down a bit into the substrate, so they do not turn or jostle. Be careful when moving them. Turning the eggs or jarring them can kill the delicate embryos.

Place the egg box on top of the bricks in the incubator and close the lid. Now, you wait. Actually, you do need to check on them every other day or so. You want to remove any obviously bad eggs, make sure the temperature and humidity are still holding, add water to the incubator if necessary, etc.

Iguana eggs hatch in an average of 90 days. Starting around the 80th day, check the eggs daily or twice a day for hatchlings.

Bringing Up Babies

When/if the eggs hatch, don't faint. Screaming, jumping up and down, and calling all of your friends and relatives are acceptable.

Iguanas often poke their heads out of their eggs before they fully emerge. They also may slit a hole in the egg and stay put for a day or two. Have patience. Taking a baby iguana out of the egg before it comes out on its own usually will kill it. Even if it doesn't die immediately, it will probably weaken and die in a few days. Let the babies come out when they are ready.

Once the babies have emerged and are moving around the egg box, you should move them to a nursery cage. A nursery cage is just like a regular cage, but with all the fixtures scaled down to baby size. You should have this cage set up for at least a week before you expect to get hatchlings. Remember that they could hatch early.

I would set up the hatchlings so that you have no more than ten in each cage. Make sure that the cage is large enough so that each baby can perch and bask. You might want to have more than one basking spot, so that smaller hatchlings are not excluded from the light.

For the first week or so after hatching, it is a good idea to keep the humidity in the nursery cage very high. Extra spraying is a good idea, as is using a humidifier.

Feed the babies as you would the adults, but chop the food finely. Everything they eat should be bite-sized. Observe them to make sure all the babies are eating, defecating, drinking, and behaving normally. Having a scale and weighing the babies every day or so will let you know if any are not eating and growing as they should.

If you've gotten to this stage, the only thing I have left to say to you about the babies is good luck finding homes for them all.

Spaying and Neutering

If you want to avoid all the troubles associated with breeding and the breeding season, you should have your iguana spayed or neutered. A good reptile vet will be familiar with this procedure and able to answer any questions you have about it.

Before deciding to have your iguana altered (another way of saying "spayed or neutered"), remember that it is a surgical procedure. It does pose a risk to your iguana's health and well-being. Most iguanas will recover from the surgery without problems, but some will not. Talk with your vet about the risks to make an informed decision.

Neutered male iguanas rarely exhibit any of the breeding behaviors discussed earlier. They do not get the orange color associated with sexed-up males. If neutered before he is full-grown, a male iguana will not get as large as an unaltered male and will show less of the secondary sexual characteristics. His dewlap, crest, and jowls will be smaller than an intact male's.

A spayed female will not develop infertile eggs and will never become egg-bound. In fact, some vets and iguana keepers recommend having adult female iguanas spayed just to avoid possible egg-binding. If a female becomes egg-bound once, the vet may recommend spaying to prevent it in the future, as a female with a history of egg-binding is likely to become egg-bound in the future.

Whether or not you spay or neuter your iguana is up to you. Get all the information you can first, so that you make an informed choice that you feel good about.

Part 4

Glossary

Acclimation

The adjustment by an animal to its surroundings when in captivity.

Agonostic Display

Any social interaction between two organisms, including mating, courtship displays, and combat.

Ancestor

The organism that gave rise to later generations/species. Older works sometimes used the term "primitive" for the ancestral organism.

Anorexia

A disorder that is characterized by cessation of feeding. It may be induced by environmental stress, physical injury, or pathogenic infection.

Antibiotic

General term for a drug that will kill or control pathogenic bacteria. Examples include penicillin, amikacin, and chloramphenicol.

Arboreal

Living among trees.

Autotomy

The ability of some lizards to lose the tail and regrow a new appendage.

Axilla

The insertion point where the humerus meets the shoulder; armpit.

Behavioral Thermoregulation

The process of controlling body temperature by moving into and out of heat/shade.

Clinal Factor

A trait that is measurably distinct from one locality to another across the range of a species. If members of a northern population are small and animal size increases as one moves south, then size would be a clinal factor.

Crepuscular

Active by dusk or dawn (See Diurnal, Nocturnal.)

Derived

Status of a trait in the descendant of an ancestral form. Also, a trait that is highly modified, not found in an ancestral form.

Desiccate

To dry out or lose water.

Distend

to spread.

Diversify

The tendency for members of a genus to evolve into forms different from each other (= speciation; = radiation). For example, monitors, though similar in general form, vary tremendously in size, pattern, snout shape, and nostril position.

Diurnal

Active during daylight hours.

Electrophoresis

A biochemical technique that uses an electric charge to separate proteins from samples of tissue in a gel. The prints formed from these tests produce highly characteristic images from which lineage and relationships may be inferred.

Enzyme

A protein catalyst that regulates the rate at which a biochemical reaction takes place. These may induce digestion, movement, and hormone production, and are themselves regulated largely by temperature and pH.

Extinction

The termination of a species as a whole. Ecologists talk about "regional extinctions" (= extirpation) to indicate loss of populations in part of the whole range of the organism.

Facultative

The ability for some organisms to alter the workings of certain physiological functions. For example, pythons incubating eggs may produce internal body heat, but do so for the period of incubation only. (See Obligate.)

Genotype

Literally, the kind of genes possessed by an organism. The genotype can be ascertained biochemically in some cases, but is physically expressed as a Phenotype (q.v.).

Genus

A taxonomic category above species and below family. A genus typically includes many species, but may contain only one (= monospecific). In a scientific name, the genus comes first and is always capitalized.

Gondwanaland

The southern super-continent of the Mesozoic Era, comprising Australia, South America, Africa, Antarctica, India, and Madagascar. (See Laurasia.)

Hemipenes

The paired male copulatory organs that are unique to squamate reptiles (lizards, snakes, and amphisbaenids).

Holotype

The single specimen used in describing a new species. Also generally called "type." If other specimens are used to embellish a type description, the rest of the series is designated as Paratypes.

Homeostasis

The physiological processes of maintaining a steady state within an organism. Reptiles try to maintain an average body temperature by behavioral thermoregulation.

Karyotype

The number and structure of chromosomes of an organism.

Laurasia

The super-continent of the Mesozoic Era (200 to 65 million years ago) that formed the northern land mass. It contained North America, Europe, and Asia.

Maori

The indigenous aboriginal peoples of New Zealand.

Metabolism

The net biochemical activity of a living organism.

Monophyletic

A group including a common ancestor and all of its descendants. This is generally considered the most natural way to assign organisms to taxonomic categories.

Morphology

The anatomy of an organism. Also, the scientific study of structure.

Neonate

A newly hatched young reptile.

Nocturnal

Active at night.

Obligate

Refers to a condition that must be fulfilled by the physiology of an organism. An obligate endotherm always produces body heat while alive and cannot stop this function by moving out of sunlight.

Opportunistic

A feeding strategy that indicates the animal will consume virtually any food item, animal or plant, dead or alive, that it encounters.

Oviparous

Egg-laying.

Ovoviviparous

Eggs are retained inside the female until birth (= parturition). Differs from true live birth (= viviparity) in that young are not nourished by the mother during the developmental period. The distinctions are subtle and may not be meaningful in some cases, so recently the term has fallen into disfavor.

Paraphyletic

A situation when existing phylogenies include only some of the descendants of a particular ancestor; such groupings are considered artificial because they do not include all descendants.

Pathogenic

Disease-causing. Examples include many viruses and bacteria.

Phenotype

The appearance of an organism. (See Genotype.)

Phylogeny

The evolutionary lineage, or history, of a group.

Protist

A single-celled living organism belonging to the kingdom Protista. The other kingdoms recognized are Monera (bacteria), Fungi, Plantae, and Animalia.

Riparian

Living on the banks of a river or stream.

Salmonella

A genus of the bacterium responsible for a digestive illness known as salmonellosis.

Secondary

A modification in evolutionary terms. Refers to an alteration from an ancestral condition. As snakes are evolved from lizards, the ancestral snakes had limbs; their loss in living snakes is a secondary adaptation.

Sexual Dimorphism

Any physical distinction between sexes of a species, including color, crest ornamentation, preanal pores, or size, for example.

Sister Group

Two or more taxa (i.e., species or genera) that share a common ancestor.

Species

A particular grouping of organisms that share numerous traits. Members of the same species share more traits than they do with other species within the same genus. In a scientific name, the species name is the second term and is never capitalized.

Substrate

The material that is on the bottom of the terrarium, such as soil, bark, newspaper, or gravel.

Systematics

The branch of biology that seeks to understand origins and relationships of organisms.

Taxonomy

That branch of systematics that assigns names to organisms.

Tripod Position

A characteristic stance assumed by many lizards, including monitors and alligator lizards, where the lizard stands upright, supported by the two hind limbs and the base of the tail.

Resources

Iguana Societies and Organizations

Green Iguana Society

E-mail: questions@greenigsociety.org

http://www.greenigsociety.org/home.html

We are dedicated to providing quality information on iguana care as well as information on current iguana adoptions and rescues throughout the United States and Canada.

International Iguana Society

133 Steele Road

West Hartford, CT 06119

E-mail: ctenosaura@cyclura.com

http://www.iguanasociety.org/

We work to secure the long-term survival of all iguanas.

The Iguana Club

http://www.theiguana.com/

Your giant green iguana information exchange.

Iguana-Related Websites

Love My Iguanas Adoption Center

(http://www.geocities.com/Petsburgh/Farm/2607/adopt.html#adoptionandrescue)

This website lists numerous reptile adoption and rescue sites across the United States. It also offers extensive information regarding iguana health and general care, with links to other iguana-related websites.

The Basking Spot

(http://www.baskingspot.com)

Known as "The Internet Spot for Herp News and Links," The Basking Spot provides an array of reptile news stories; information on care; and links to various societies and organizations, educational sites, and rescue, rehabilitation, and adoption information.

The Iguana Den

(http://www.iguanaden.com/main.htm)
This comprehensive website examines
issues such as iguana housing, health, care,
and adoption.

Iguana-Related Publications

Iguana Iguana Newsletter

23852 Pacific Coast Highway, Ste. 123
Malibu, CA 90265
E-mail: info@windgrafix.com
http://www.iguana-news.com/

Iguana Times Journal

Iguana Times Back Issues
International Iguana Society, Inc.
Dept. WS
133 Steele Road
West Hartford, CT 06119
http://www.iguanasociety.org/backIssues/
BackIssuesIndex.html

Reptilian Magazine

P.O. Box 1006
Southhampton
Hampshire
SO19 7TS
United Kingdom
E-mail: Info@cviewmedia.com
http://www.cviewmedia.com/

Veterinary Specialty/Membership Organizations

Association of Reptilian and Amphibian Veterinarians (ARAV)

P.O. Box 605
Chester Heights, PA 19017
Phone: (610) 358-9530
E-mail: ARAVETS@aol.com
http://www.arav.org/

Herp Vet Connection

E-mail: sue@herpvetconnection.com
http://www.herpvetconnection.com/

Animal Welfare Groups and Organizations

American Society for the Prevention of Cruelty to Animals (ASPCA)

424 E. 92nd Street

New York, NY 10128-6804

Phone: (212) 876-7700

http://www.aspca.org

The Humane Society of the United States (HSUS)

2100 L Street, NW

Washington DC 20037

Phone: (202) 452-1100

http://www.hsus.org

Index

Photo Credits

A. Both, 30

A. Del Prete, 19, 98

C. Foltz, 14, 45, 95

I. Francais, 11-12, 17, 22, 25-26, 34-35, 41, 49, 53, 60, 74, 76, 81, 86, 101-102, 110, 120, 128, 135, 153-154, 157-158

J. Balzarini, 141

J. Prime, 61-64, 83-84, 90, 119, 122, 167

J.C. Tyson, 57, 127

M. Gilroy, 65

M. Walls, 13, 29, 111-112, 115-116, 121, 142-143, 155, 170-171

P. Keeler, 131

Susan Webb (courtesy of Animal Kingdom), 23, 139, 149

TFH Archives, 24, 85, 109

U.E. Friese, 21

W.P. Mara, 27, 51, 151

Cartoons by Michael Pifer